Reviving the Industrial City

Jerry A. Webman

Reviving the Industrial City

The Politics of Urban Renewal
in Lyon and Birmingham

Rutgers University Press
New Brunswick · New Jersey

Set in 11 on 13½ point Caledonia type
Manufactured in the United States of America

Library of Congress Cataloging in Publication Data

Webman, Jerry A., 1949–
  Reviving the industrial city.
  Bibliography: p.
  Includes index.
  1. Urban renewal—France—Lyon. 2. Urban renewal—
England—Birmingham (West Midlands). 3. Urban policy—
France—Case studies. 4. Urban policy—England—Case
studies. I. Title.
HT178.F72L978   307.7'6   81–21137
ISBN 0–8135–0947–5   AACR2

To my mother
and the memory of my father

Contents

Acknowledgments

This research was supported by grants from the Institution for Social and Policy Studies and the Concilium of International and Area Studies of Yale University and the Council on the Social Sciences and Humanities of Princeton University.

I am indebted to the politicians, administrators, and scholars whose willingness to spend time answering my questions and challenges made this study possible. I am additionally grateful to my eating and drinking companions in both Lyon and Birmingham who added a richness and humaneness to my research efforts and, I hope, to the product of those efforts.

I profited greatly from the generous intellectual support of numerous friends and colleagues. Help with research, analytic, and stylistic problems came from many sources at many crucial points. Among those who offered assistance on one or more of these occasions were Joseph LaPalombara, who acted as adviser during the original research project, David Bradford, David Cameron, Michael Danielson, Mattei Dogan, James Fesler, Stanley Greenberg, Judith Gruber, Juan Linz, David Mayhew, Edward Pauly, Robert Rich, Arthur Stein, Ezra Suleiman, Kenneth Wald, and Douglas Yates. Reviewers for Rutgers University Press added acute, helpful criticism and advice.

Gerard Bamet, François Chazel, François d'Arcy, Douglas Hart, and James Sharpe offered important guidance with the field research. Estelle Brodkey, Albert Eng, Vivian Laska, Gail Marcus, and Jonathan Moore helped prepare grant proposals and the final manuscript. Marlie Wasserman and Barbara Westergaard subjected the text to invaluable editorial scrutiny. Mavis Hoesly patiently deciphered and typed the manuscript.

Portions of Chapters 1 and 2 previously appeared in *Comparative Politics*. The editors of that journal have kindly allowed this material to be reprinted here.

My greatest debt, however, is to Susan Ginsburg Webman, who brought the whole project into perspective.

Final responsibility remains my own.

LYON
Urban Renewal Sites

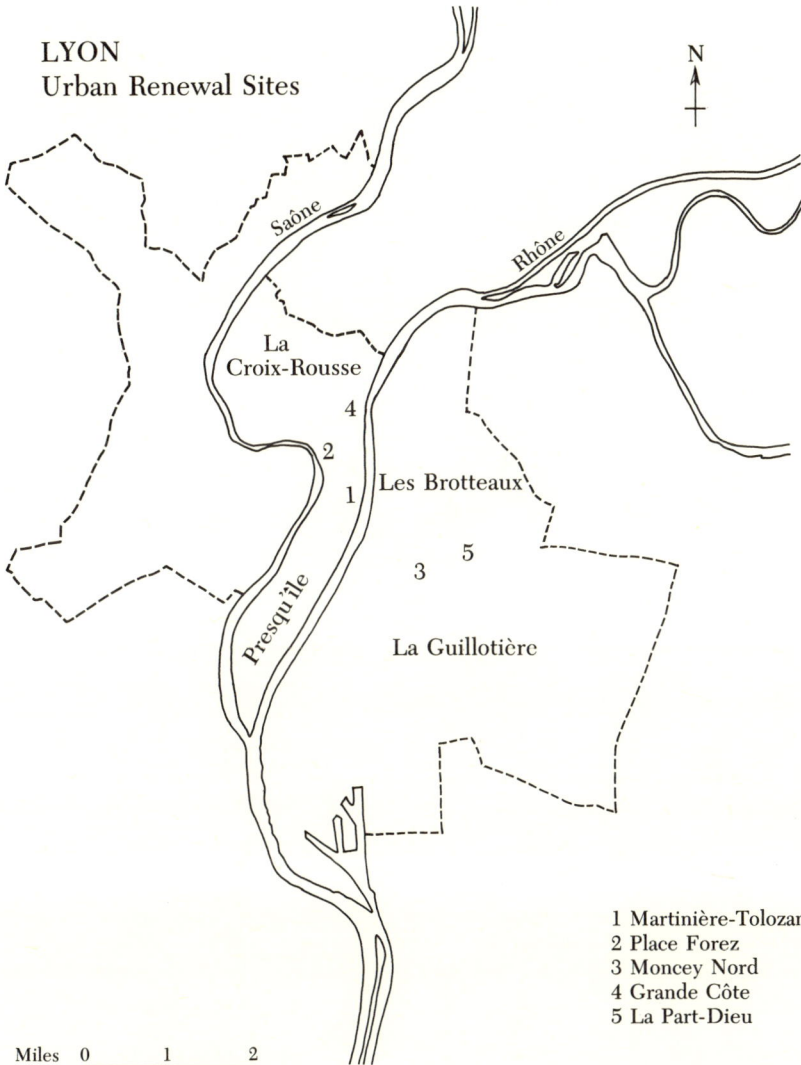

N

Saône

Rhône

La
Croix-Rousse

4

2

1   Les Brotteaux

Presqu'île

5

3

La Guillotière

1 Martinière-Tolozan
2 Place Forez
3 Moncey Nord
4 Grande Côte
5 La Part-Dieu

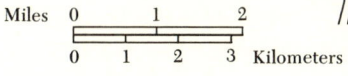

Miles   0   1   2

0   1   2   3   Kilometers

BIRMINGHAM
Urban Renewal Sites

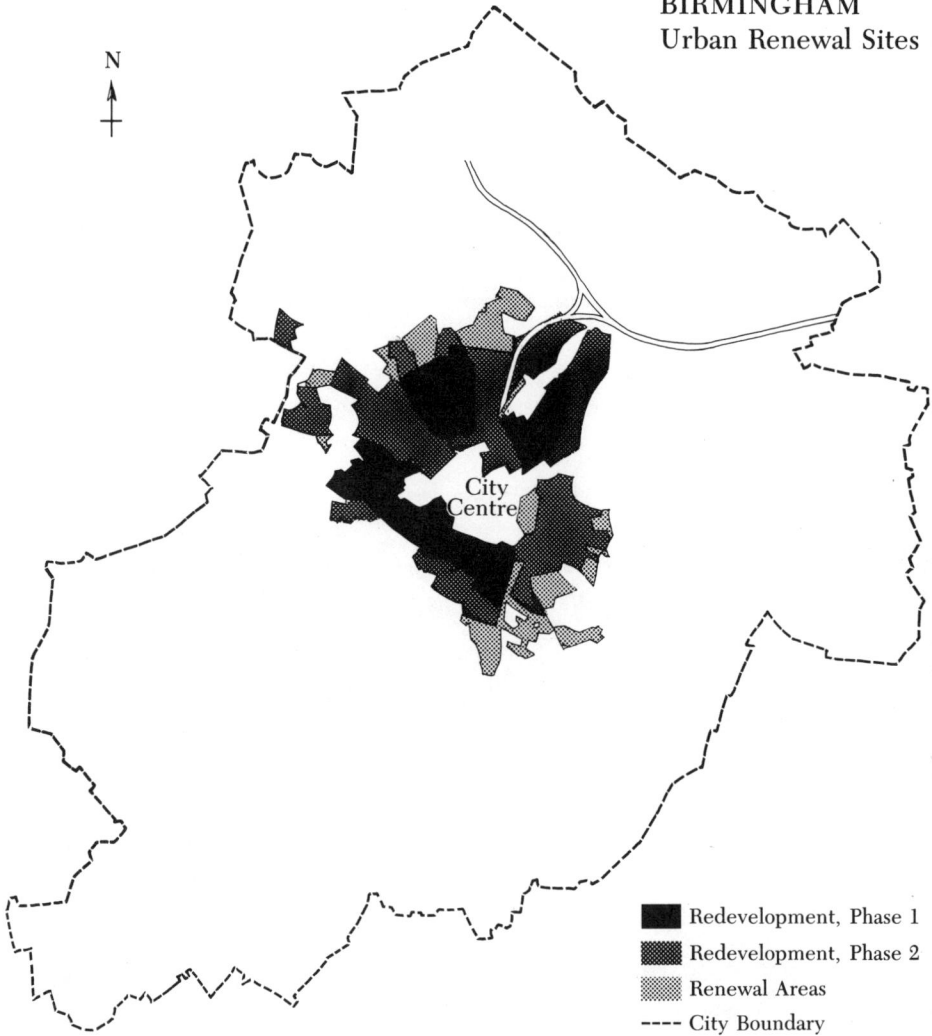

N

City
Centre

■ Redevelopment, Phase 1
▨ Redevelopment, Phase 2
▦ Renewal Areas
--- City Boundary

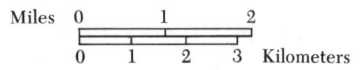

Miles 0   1   2
       0   1   2   3   Kilometers

Public Control and the Aging City

1

Urban Redevelopment in Lyon and Birmingham

In the decade that followed World War II, governments through-out Western Europe and North America adopted and began to implement major programs designed to revive and reshape the man-made environment of their older cities. Whether spurred on by extensive wartime destruction or simply by the accumulation of deteriorated neighborhoods and their associated social ills, planners and politicians began offering the dream of replacing existing slums and blighted areas with orderly, healthful, modern cities.

Although these redevelopment efforts often began with similar mixtures of crowded, badly deteriorated housing, dirty, obsolete industry, and decaying commercial centers, they produced widely varying results. In some cities, the narrow streets and small shops of the central business district gave way to shopping malls and parking garages. In others, decaying neighborhoods were upgraded by projects that made the housing more attractive to higher-income families or that made land available to prestigious institutions like universities and medical and cultural centers. Sometimes slums were replaced with modern housing intended for residents with the same income levels as former inhabitants, at other times with expressways and sports arenas. Occasionally chaotic layouts gave way to bold, orderly designs, but more often the original plans were ignored, continuously changed, or left half completed.[1]

Despite this wide variation in outcomes, two common assumptions connected all these programs:[2] (1) that because owners of urban property lack incentives to coordinate their investment decisions in a mutually advantageous way, cities decline faster and adapt to changing conditions more slowly than physical and economic obsolescence and opportunities would dictate, and (2) that governments can draw up and impose development plans to ensure that designated urban areas will enjoy a coordinated program of public and private investment to revive these declining cities. I consider the first assumption and the programmatic connection between the two assumptions below. Before doing so I would like to point out that the second theme raises an issue for public policy that goes well beyond the revitalization of older cities.

Policy Coherence: The Synoptic Ideal

Coordinated, coherent, consistent policymaking stands out as an ideal among those who see the potential for collective solutions to social ills of many kinds. Even people presumably chastened by considerable personal experience with the complex and contradictory processes of carrying out governmental programs find themselves longing for public action that "seeks to respond to the system in its entirety," rather than "to a single part of the system."[3] This longing for holistic planning and expert analysis free from political interference C. E. Lindblom calls the "synoptic aspiration."[4]

No area of public policy has a monopoly on synoptic aspirations. They are present when the author of a careful study of how American foreign policy is made assumes that American influence outside its borders should be "exercised by coordinated government actions which support conscious, central United States policy purposes."[5] The same ideal moved a presidential urban policy task force to write, "The magnitude of our urban problems and the fact that billions of dollars are now spent on our cities, often in an uncoordinated way, make a comprehensive national urban policy essential."[6] Nor are such appeals bound by place or political system. Witness a 1971 report of the Communist Party of the Soviet Union that called for "integrating development" in urban areas and "coordinating the work of enterprises and organizations of different departmental subordination," but then indicated that just the opposite was occurring.[7] Examples of the goal are not difficult to find; examples of its realization are, as several of the urban renewal examples suggest. If the ideal is commonly recognized, why is it rarely put into practice? Why do governments rarely act with coherence and consistency? Under what conditions are they most likely to do so?

This study provides a political answer to those questions. To do so, it uses urban redevelopment's emphasis on planned, publicly directed urban change to ask what political conditions made the implementation of policies of this sort possible. To compare policymaking under substantially different political conditions, eight redevelopment projects in two aging industrial cities, Birmingham in the English Midlands and Lyon in southeastern France, are considered. Among these projects are instances of relative success and relative failure in achieving coherent governmental action. I argue that these differences are neither accidents nor the result of varying attention to planning but that they follow from enduring differences in the way the two cities are governed.

The analysis begins by describing the particular approach to urban redevelopment employed in France, Great Britain, and the United States. This discussion of the programs makes it possible to describe their political demands more specifically and then to ask under what conditions these demands could be met.

Urban Redevelopment

Cities decline for at least as many reasons as they grow. Sometimes governments have encouraged decline, sometimes opposed it, sometimes ignored it. The wave of urban renewal programs mentioned above was a response to a particular pattern of decline and a particular analysis of the causes of that decline. The cities in these examples—Liverpool, New Haven, Chicago, the eastern edges of Paris—grew with the Industrial Revolution and the concentrations of industry and humanity it engendered. These same cities began to lose enterprises and people as advances in production and transportation technology transformed their high densities from an asset to a liability. New investment occurred elsewhere; workers and managers, who had already begun settling urban fringe areas, followed the new investment. As a result, factories, houses, and commercial areas, some already badly war-torn, were abandoned or converted to uses that produced lower prices, lower rents, lower wages, and thus still lower levels of investment. So continued the classic cycle of urban decline.[8]

This cyclic pattern of obsolescence, disinvestment, and further obsolescence suggested to those who framed urban renewal programs that the revival of cities demanded a strategy with high synoptic ideals. If the new investment in housing, industry, and commerce, which was certainly occurring in the industrialized countries, could be directed toward existing cities, then the cycle could be broken. The reason that investment went elsewhere, so the argument went, lay in the cycle itself and in the logic of private investment decision making. Concerted public action was the obvious solution.

In his analysis of urban renewal in New Haven, Robert Dahl spells out this analysis:

> A city constantly undergoes change of some sort. But piecemeal changes often merely reduce some tensions while they generate others. As in the classic case of the onset of an economic depression, when the actions each individual businessman takes to save his own skin by laying off employees and living off inventories only speeds the depression on its way, so in the case of the city, the sum total of piecemeal actions may end up creating a city that very few people would choose to design if they were capable of anticipating a wider range of consequences and had some means of avoiding these consequences without immediate loss.[9]

The collective preference, in other words, of those who live, work, and own property in cities may be quite different from the sum of their individual, independently expressed preferences for the matters they can themselves control. Yet few people will make obvious sacrifices for common goals if others are free to pursue their clear self-interest unless, of course, public authority requires such sacrifices.

Dahl expresses a general rationale for planned urban development. An extension of the same argument leads to a dilemma that connects unplanned change with forces that accelerate urban decline.

As a property owner, I know that the value of my neighbor's property increases simply because I improve my own and that I will profit from my neighbor's investments even if I do nothing at all. Furthermore, my return will be diminished if I fix up my property and my neighbor fails to improve his. Unsure of each other's intentions we have an incentive therefore to sit tight, hope that our neighbor will provide a windfall, and avoid risking more of our own capital. Thus we do nothing to upgrade our neighborhood although we would both be better off if we could agree to make equivalent improvements and find a way to force each other to uphold that agreement.[10] In principle a clever developer might see the opportunities my neighbor and I have missed, buy our property, and improve it. Given, however, the "very heavy transaction and bargaining costs of large-scale land assembly,"[11] private investors are unlikely to offer the comprehensive solutions that this problem demands once it is extended to a sizable urban area. The result is accelerated disinvestment and decline in areas that might be made attractive for new growth.

If investment decisions for such urban areas could be coordinated and controlled uniformly, the dilemma could be resolved, and an increased, socially beneficial level of investment achieved. This resolution is the principal goal of public urban renewal programs. In these programs the government, rather than individual landlords, tenants, buyers, and sellers, would decide on the level of maintenance of urban sites. The resulting concentration of public authority and financial resources would allow planned investment decisions to be made simultaneously for large areas. Everyone would invest because everyone else invested.

In practice government can impose such a plan by subsidizing private investment in a defined urban area but requiring that this investment conform to an overall design. Government can further ensure this planned development by assembling and improving sites and upgrading public infrastructure. The strategy's keystone is the use of public authority to unify investment decisions for a specified area so that they all serve a common plan. With some significant variations, which are discussed in the context of specific projects, the French and British (American as well)[12] urban renewal programs have been based on just this strategy.[13]

This appeal to the state to ensure a collective response to urban problems, to realize in other words the synoptic ideal, has firm roots in liberal political thought, but it begs two important questions which complicate this simple solution. First of all, the tendency of atomistic investment decisions to produce a city "very few people would choose to design" does not imply that some collective decision will produce a city all *but* a few people would choose to design. A solution to the investment dilemma may benefit the owners of property in a particular area but impose costs upon renters of the improved property or owners of property outside the redevelopment area. To assume, therefore, that the "right" collective solution simply increases efficiency and general welfare is to ignore the unequal distribution of costs and benefits such plans produce.

Those who must pay these costs, however, are less likely to ignore them. The consequence is that plans that appear neutral to planners engender controversy among those who must live with their results. These controversies do not derive from failure to consider all relevant parties in creating plans but, in fact, reflect more fundamental conflicts over the interests governmental action should serve and over the ways cities and their economic functions should develop. The result, of course, is politics.

A second unanswered question follows from these conflicts and controversies. A collective redevelopment plan is a solution to the dilemma of joint action if and to the extent that a public takeover of investment decisions in fact unifies and concentrates the making of those decisions. The economic analysis of urban redevelopment begs this question of governmental effectiveness in planning because it assumes that government can routinely be regarded as a unitary actor, which can make complex decisions coherently and carry them out consistently.

But this unity of purpose and action cannot be assumed if we are concerned with the content of urban redevelopment policy. As Hugh Heclo has written, "Social policy is not like a shoe or a loaf of bread; it is too complex to be explained simply as the predicate of some 'maker.'"[14] Public action will reflect the diversity of those whose combined and conflicting actions make it occur. It may even reflect concessions to those who object to anything occurring at all. The redevelopment strategy demands synopsis; governmental action does not ensure that synopsis will ensue.

Political Structure

To point to this uncertainty and variability in the extent to which a redevelopment plan—regardless of content—will be carried out is simply to say that the fulfillment of plans is a political matter. The conflict is evident. On the one hand redevelopment programs and those who plan their implementation pursue a design for coordinated development. On the other hand those whose interests are affected by those plans seek changes to serve their special concerns. The battle, as almost any case study of urban renewal will show, takes place not just over the adoption of a renewal plan but over the many coordinated public and private actions that must occur if the plan's provisions are to be fulfilled.

The outcome of these battles—the degree to which the results of public action look like the plan—will depend on the ability of those who advocate the holistic design to achieve and maintain more political support than those who demand changes. Alan Altshuler has described the political requisite: "If there are important conflicts of interest in a society that cannot be resolved to the advantage of all parties, then planners require the guidance of a strong political arbiter."[15] The degree to which city governments pursue comprehensive plans for urban change, Altshuler argues, depends less on the planners than on the existence of "a coherent 'power elite' firmly committed to a plan."[16] The political arbiter's role is not simply to bless the plan but to enforce compliance with its provisions through the many controversies it must endure. In carrying out planned redevelopment three issues are especially important for this city hall Leviathan:

1. At a minimum, coherent public action implies the coordination of public agencies whose special expertise, resources, and authority are required for planned intervention. But coordination presumes a common goal; such agencies are likely to hold firmly to differing views about desirable outcomes, and coincidence of view would indeed be coincidental. Can the arbiter secure commitment to a common objective?

2. A coordinated plan is not coordinated action. The internal views of and the external pressures on these agencies will change over time, especially as the financial, psychological, and political costs of redevelopment become apparent. Can the arbiter keep everyone in line as commitments grow less palatable?

3. Although redevelopment is based on public determination of investment decisions, some of those decisions will be carried out by private firms and households, free at least to withhold action in redevelopment areas. Will the assumed arbiter have the authority or the incentives to channel private action toward redevelopment plans or to substitute public action for private inaction?

Where affirmative answers can be given to such questions, political conditions are relatively favorable for planned redevelopment. The analytical problem is to understand the conditions under which such an arbiter can emerge. The argument that follows explores the importance of what I refer to as political structure for the development of this firm political support for planned redevelopment. By political structure I mean the enduring formal and informal rules by which collective decisions are reached and enacted in a particular place, like Birmingham or Lyon. These rules name the key actors in a political system, the resources those actors will deploy, and the expectations they will hold of one another.

Two points must be stressed. First, political structure comes before and remains after redevelopment projects are proposed and executed. Large, controversial programs may bring changes in the political rules, but political structure will be part of the landscape in which redevelopment takes place. Second, resources, rules, and expectations are not easily seen. What can be seen are the public and private organizations that hold the expectations, follow the rules, and control the resources and are thus in a position to affect the outcome of public policy.

This formulation implies that the key to the politics of redevelopment in a particular urban area is an understanding of the interests and the relative importance for redevelopment programs of the most important political organizations. Knowing these components of political structure, we know which views are most likely to be reflected in the content of redevelopment programs, and we know the likelihood that any one organization will serve as political arbiter and enforce the ideal of planning. Political organizations—parties, administrative agencies, voluntary associations, corporations—and their behavior are thus the basis for explanation in the analysis that follows.[17]

Of particular importance are the characteristics of political structure that tend either to concentrate or to fragment influence over the execution of redevelopment projects. We want to find out whether the emergence of a political arbiter depends on the concentration of political control in a small number of political organizations or if some kinds of concentration are more important than others. To do so, I focus on three features of urban governance, each of which provides a potential or reputed source of control over public policy, and gauge its effect on planned urban change.

The first of these sources is the central government. To what extent does it intervene in making policy for provincial cities? Important literature in American political science suggests that political centralization of the sort associated with France leads to effective urban policymaking. The discussion in Chapter 2 raises questions about both the premise and the extent of French centralization.

The second source of control is local organizations that attempt to contain the immediate and powerful conflicts that arise over the use of urban land. Lyon and Birmingham offer contrasts between the highly partisan image of British municipal politics and the dual French image of mayoral leadership and technocratic approaches to policy conflicts. Again, conclusions in Chapter 3 about the effectiveness of the institutions concerned cast doubt on the usual accounts of how they operate.

The third source of control is public agencies empowered to plan for private investment. The issue here returns to the fundamental premise of redevelopment programs. Complete public control over private investment is rarely asserted in these redevelopment projects. More usual is a mixture of public and private action. The "French model" of "indicative," democratic planning would suggest that an effective mechanism exists in that country for the direction of private purposes toward public goals. Chapter 4 asks whether such a model provides a means of control for redevelopment programs.

These three sources of control and the fragmentation with which they attempt to deal thus provide the basis for an analysis of the effects of variation in political structure on synoptic policymaking. In addition the discussion leads to revised images of domestic policymaking in France and Great Britain. And finally, the conclusions in fact question the appropriateness of synoptic policymaking as a goal for public action.

To compare the effects of variation in these three elements of political structure on the content of urban redevelopment projects in Lyon and Birmingham, I consider three characteristics of specific projects. First, to assess the amount of control over

policymaking that any public agency actually achieved, I ask
how much projects changed between their official adoption and
their completion or termination. Was a publicly promulgated
plan imposed holistically on a sector of the city or was the original scheme cut apart and reformed as implementation proceeded? Second, to measure the extent of this control within the
two cities, I compare the physical size of projects and the kinds
of areas where projects were carried out. Finally, to estimate the
potential for conflict engendered by the projects, I compare the
general use of land within the project area before and after
redevelopment.

The primary source of data for this study is 101 loosely structured interviews conducted between April 1974 and May 1975
and in June and July of 1978 with political leaders and observers
knowledgeable about urban renewal in the two cities. My informants fit seven basic categories: local politicians (current office-
holders, aspirants to office, and retired officeholders), local professional and administrative officials, journalists and scholars
with special knowledge of the two cities, officials of central government field offices responsible for Birmingham and Lyon (Department of the Environment in Birmingham, the Ministère de
l'Equipement et du logement, the Organisation d'Etude d'aménagement d'aires métropolitaine de Lyon, the Société centrale
pour l'Equipement du territoire,[18] and the prefecture in Lyon),
community organizers and neighborhood defense-group leaders, central party officials (the British Labour and Conservative
parties only), and central ministry officials. The informants provided information about their relationships with one another,
accounts of decision-making processes, and descriptions of completed, projected, and abandoned urban renewal projects.

Several of these men and women also let me look at their urban redevelopment files. Where informants permitted, these
private documents are cited; in other cases I have treated material from these files as if derived from interviews. Other docu-
mentary sources are published.

To an extent this study is bound by the particular time and places in which it was conducted; to a larger extent it is not. Some specific aspects of the redevelopment programs—the emphasis on wholesale clearance, for example—have changed in both countries since the mid-1970s. Similarly the political structures of the two cities have changed as some pressures on the systems have grown and others diminished and as groups have gained and lost power. Consequently, to the extent that urban renewal continues, in neither Lyon nor Birmingham is it conducted in 1982 as it was in 1952 or 1972. The argument that follows, however, does not apply solely to the specific programs these two cities pursued during a certain period. Instead it applies to a general strategy for effecting urban change and to the political requisites of carrying out such a strategy. The political conditions necessary to comprehensive urban planning will change even more slowly than will political structures in Lyon and Birmingham.

Birmingham and Lyon:
The Legacy of the Industrial Revolution

Birmingham and Lyon are, by resolution of their respective city councils, "twinned cities." This twinning means a special place for Birmingham's products in Lyon's trade fair, ceremonial exchanges among city dignitaries, and reciprocal visits by community groups from both cities. For present purposes, it suggests the recognition of several important similarities between the two cities. Both are the second city in their respective countries[19] and, during the period under consideration here, remained heavily industrial: about 45 percent of the labor force of metropolitan Lyon is employed in manufacture and construction;[20] the comparable figure for Birmingham is just over 50 percent.[21] Both cities have experienced a continuing substantial demand on their housing market.[22]

Both cities also owe their size and importance to rapid growth during the Industrial Revolution. Birmingham, which had only

15,000 residents in 1700,[23] had grown to 74,000 in 1801, 233,000 in 1851, and 523,000 by 1900.[24] Lyon, a much more important medieval and Renaissance center than Birmingham,[25] grew only from 110,000 inhabitants in 1800 to 177,000 in 1850, but reached 323,000 by 1861 and 459,000 in 1900. [26]

In both cases this rapid growth was concentrated in dense, poorly built industrial quarters. In Birmingham the bulk of the growth occurred in a mixed industrial and residential band surrounding the original city center.[27] In Lyon two areas accommodated the expanding population. The Croix-Rousse, in the hills north of the city center, grew from 6,000 to 19,000 inhabitants between 1800 and 1851,[28] while the Guillotière, formerly a village on the Rhone's left bank, grew from 10,000 inhabitants in 1829 to 78,000 by 1876 and 145,000 in 1896.[29]

As a result of these periods of expansion, both cities found themselves by the middle of the twentieth century with vast residential areas that were substandard by contemporary views. One study found that in the Croix-Rousse "two-thirds of the apartments have only one or two rooms and do not possess interior sanitary facilities"; densities reached 194 persons per acre.[30] A careful postwar study of Birmingham's housing stock called 27 percent "structurally unsound" and "ripe for demolition."[31] Densities in these sections of Birmingham were between 150 and 180 persons per acre.[32] To exacerbate the problems of overcrowding, many of the buildings in these areas were cheaply built by standards of their own day, with inadequate ventilation, no sanitary facilities, and flimsy construction.[33]

Finally, these buildings were simply old. Before redevelopment programs began to have an effect, 66 percent of Lyon's housing[34] and 59 percent of Birmingham's[35] predated World War I.

By the late 1940s, in short, significant areas of both cities had experienced the cycle of urban disinvestment and decline considered earlier in general terms. The existing structures were deteriorated and getting worse, and yet the land, located in each case near the center of a thriving city, seemed intrinsically valu-

able. With no prospect that private investors could or would reverse the trend toward decay, redevelopment programs joined
the agenda of public action.

Both cities did indeed act. In the thirty years following World
War II, both Lyon and Birmingham launched major programs
of public investment and publicly guided private investment
aimed at a major restructuring of the cities' older industrial
areas. Starting at quite similar points with quite similar stated
goals, these programs left the two cities significantly changed,
but changed in very different ways.

Birmingham: Comprehensive Redevelopment and Urban Renewal

Sir Herbert Manzoni, Birmingham's long-time (1935–1963)
city surveyor and chief engineer and author of the city's redevelopment programs, described in the following manner a
strategy that was to characterize Birmingham's urban redevelopment efforts for two and a half decades. According to Manzoni
prewar projects had dealt with small isolated groups of slum
houses: "This was leading to a very patchy sort of development
along existing road patterns, and was most unsatisfactory. About
1936, therefore, the idea of a much more comprehensive redevelopment was examined. As a result it was found that if a
large individual area of very old property could be dealt with in
its entirety, a complete redesign of the roads would allow it to be
resuscitated in a modern way with considerable economy of
space."[36] "The scheme, however," wrote Manzoni to the city
council, "can only be carried out as a whole and it involves complete acquisition of all the existing site and buildings, except the
industrial premises in the factory areas."[37] Although Manzoni
referred in these statements to one initial area of 263 acres and
5,277 dwellings,[38] the approach he outlined eventually led to a
twenty-five-year program that restructured a doughnut of nearly
3,000 acres around the city center.

A recent and critical municipal report has described this huge
project:

In 1944, before the end of the Second World War, the city took
advantage of the Town and Country Planning Act of 1944 (The
Blitz and the Blight Act) to acquire practically all the land adjacent
to the city centre and comprising in total some 1,100 acres. . . .
Almost every building was demolished, including 30,000 houses,
3,900 shops and 2,300 industrial and commercial premises. They
have been completely rebuilt to new road patterns with schools,
open space, housing, shopping and the facilities for a complete
community.

    The second phase of the redevelopment commenced in 1968.
. . . There were 16 of these areas [1,800 acres] [39] and the work will
include the demolition of 29,318 houses. [40]

Coupled with the construction of 87,784 municipally owned
housing units in redeveloped, vacant, and suburban fringe
areas,[41] Comprehensive Redevelopment included over 20 percent of Birmingham's households.

    Initial plans for five redevelopment areas passed the Birming-
ham Council in early 1946 and the Ministry of Town and Country Planning by the middle of the next year. An additional six-
teen smaller areas were approved in 1955. Although authorities
recognized from the beginning that they would require two or
three decades to fulfill their plans, they had laid down a synoptic
solution to the problem of central city decline.[42]

    To a remarkable extent these plans were fulfilled. If project
designs from the early 1950s for the five initial redevelopment
areas could be blown up to life-size, they would fit nicely on top
of the present-day neighborhoods. Architects found that anticipated densities of 130 persons per acre could not be reached
even with extensive use of high-rise buildings, but the extent
and use of the areas (for low-income housing) remained unaltered between initial plans and actual results. With an exception to be noted, the same may be said of the second phase of
redevelopment.

    High-level Birmingham officials had anticipated and pro-
moted a third phase of Comprehensive Redevelopment (this
time for areas to include some 10,000 dwellings) until 1972 when

the strategy changed drastically. New voices questioned and rejected the idea that an area must be "dealt with in its entirety"
or that a "scheme can only be carried out as a whole." By 1974,
when politicians spoke of a "sudden reversal"[43] of Comprehensive Redevelopment, a very different approach to redevelopment was under way.

The new approach still recognized the problem of decayed
inner-city areas, which the anticipated third phase of redevelopment had identified. The city, however, turned to a program (for
what were subsequently called Renewal Areas) with a very different strategy. "It is in the twenty-eight Renewal Areas," wrote
Birmingham's urban renewal officer, "that the immediate problems of the rapidly deteriorating properties and environment
and the consequent social problems require urgent and active
treatment if demolition and clearance [are] to be avoided. The
majority of the properties could be classified as unfit and these
areas would undoubtedly have been the next generation of redevelopment areas."[44] With this new strategy, wholesale clearance is no longer a policy goal; it is a consequence that public
action seeks to avoid.

The name "Urban Renewal" is applied to a series of programs
adopted by the Birmingham City Council in 1973, but it is of
interest here as it applies to areas included in plans for the
third phase of redevelopment. Action in those areas rested on
three pillars. First, administration of renewal efforts would be
based on downtown and neighborhood-level interdepartmental
teams. Second, "people, whose lives and homes are intimately
affected"[45] would participate directly in planning efforts. And
finally, demolition decisions would be made by vote of neighborhood and block organizations. The contrast is striking: redevelopment seeks to treat large areas of the city holistically, as indivisible projects in which the city's aggregative policy process
pays attention only to general structural considerations; Urban
Renewal seeks to build on an existing physical and social structure by judging the merits of specific cases individually.

Contrasts in the execution of the program were equally striking. The Environmental Health Department, which was charged with overseeing Urban Renewal, counted almost 13,000 residential properties within the renewal areas as eligible for improvement grants. By July 1978, after five years of Urban Renewal, only 2,180 grant applications had been filed. Another 1,466 properties, 549 of which the city owned, had their scheduled improvements completed.[46] With a few notable exceptions, little of the renovation work, either completed or planned, was grouped or coordinated as renewal plans had projected. Planning had become less comprehensive, implementation still less so.

Lyon: *Coup par Coup* Redevelopment

A summary report of extensive studies conducted in Lyon by the Ministère de la Reconstruction in the mid-1950s argued the need to "reclaim sectors of the inner city that are underused or deteriorated,"[47] and listed several sections of the industrial left bank—the Brotteaux, the Guillotière, the Part-Dieu, and the Tonkin in the neighboring commune of Villeurbanne—and the Croix-Rousse as the primary examples.[48] This proposal grew out of the view that Lyon needed "to face up both to a tardiness in the modernization of the city and in the facilities of its public services and to the new needs resulting from economic expansion and the growth of the metropolitan area."[49] As we shall see, these concerns led Lyon to carry out a series of urban redevelopment projects that changed the face of several of its declining neighborhoods.

The Ministère de la Reconstruction study assigned first priority to two projects, Moncey Nord and the Part-Dieu, both located in the center of the left bank and both focused around a major existing structure.[50] Moncey Nord was the first to become operational with the cession to the city of a large, dilapidated home for the aged. That acquisition was soon supplemented by purchase of an additional 11.8 acres of surrounding small, aging residential buildings. The chief of Lyon's Public Works Department remembered: "These were mostly one-story, ground-level houses and the Cité Rambaud—a charity home for old people.

It was very deteriorated, as was everything around it. Bad. There was nothing to conserve." Original plans called for complete clearance of the acquired area, but substantial portions remained untouched by 1969 when the city terminated the project. And, as anticipated,[51] no former resident found housing in the vastly upgraded new construction.[52]

The project at Moncey Nord was to be overshadowed, however, by its neighbor, the most ambitious redevelopment project Lyon has undertaken. Well before the expansion of the city engulfed the left bank, the French cavalry had established a ninety-nine-acre parade ground and barracks on the then periphery of Lyon at the Part-Dieu. Surrounded by the modest houses and small workshops of the Guillotière, the barracks in the mid-1950s attracted the attention not only of ministry officials, but also of Lyon's aggressive new mayor. Following his election in 1958, Louis Pradel called the redevelopment of the Part-Dieu one of "two great projects that I would like to see get under way."[53]

As part of the 1958 agreement under which the government agreed to sell the land to Lyon, 3.8 acres were reserved for a state administrative center; the remainder of the site would be devoted to some 2,800 housing units and to sufficient schools, parks, and shops to serve them and their immediate neighbors.[54] By early 1960, when the municipal council approved an overall design, the state's share had doubled, and another five acres had been allocated to the national radio network.[55] Some 2,000 low- and middle-income housing units remained.[56]

Although the army concluded the sale of its real estate in 1958, it demanded nearly ten years to vacate, section by section. The first section became available in 1961, and work soon began on two Le Corbusier-style *"barres"* containing 800 relatively costly apartments and on the Maison de la Radio. These buildings were to be the only completed elements from the original plans.

After considerable delay and discussion, work began again in 1968. The project had expanded to include land cleared from the

Moncey Nord project and twenty additional acres of typical Guillotière housing cleared to the south of the military site,[57] and it had greatly changed. None of the remaining housing— much of which was to be low-income apartments—would be built.[58] Instead, land would be sold to private developers to build some two million square feet of office space and a one-million- square-foot shopping center. Together with government offices, headquarters for the metropolitan administration (the Commu- nauté urbaine), and several public enterprises, these installa- tions would make the Part-Dieu the new "Centre directionnel" of Lyon.

Although the availability of major chunks of easily cleared land became a prime motive for urban renewal on the left bank, no clear motivation appears to have affected the Croix-Rousse. Only one publicly supported project had been completed by mid-1978 in the sector, at the Place Forez. While major slum clearance projects in Lyon always seemed to involve a complete change of population, the Place Forez project was a nationally funded experiment (one of seven throughout France) with hous- ing improvement aimed at avoiding these dislocations.[59] In ac- cord with ministry regulations, a private, voluntary organization, the Association de Restauration immobilière (the Association for Building Restoration, or ARIM, established in October 1967), conducted studies of the twenty-nine buildings in the three-acre site and presented landlords with repair schedules for structural deficiencies in sanitary facilities, floors, roofing, stairways, and the like. The landlords were required to make repairs, to pay for ARIM's making them, or to sell their holdings. By accord with the Conseil municipal, the city's expropriation powers would serve to force action from refractory landlords. Finally, ARIM could arrange advantageous loans for improvements and for moderate rent increases.[60]

Although the Place Forez project is an interesting attempt at upgrading a neighborhood without disrupting it, the project is most notable because it is minor. First, the affected area itself was small: twenty-nine buildings, 457 rental units, and 854 residents.[61] Second, success and failure were almost evenly mixed: twenty buildings were improved, two buildings were demolished by the city, and seven were offered for sale, but remained unsold and thus unimproved—the city being unwilling and ARIM unable to undertake the work. Moreover, no provisions existed for environmental work such as parking facilities. Third, the experiment was nearly unique; ARIM has undertaken only one similar project in Lyon, in an old but fashionable neighborhood abutting the city center.

The report issued in 1961 by the Ministère de la Construction (until the completion of the post–World War II rebuilding, the Ministère de la Reconstruction) listed one Croix-Rousse area among eight potential urban renewal projects, albeit the last in priority: the Martinière-Tolozan sector that borders on the northern edge of the Presqu'île city center.[62] Initial plans, drawn by the Atelier d'Urbanisme and delegated to the city's construction corporation, received municipal council and ministry approval in the late 1960s. Two and eight-tenths acres of dense housing, small businesses, and silk-weaving shops would be cleared to provide space for a metro station, an east-west expressway, and modern apartment buildings, all carefully designed to blend with the steep slopes of the Croix-Rousse.

Those plans now lie in the Atelier d'Urbanisme's inactive files. The government ruled in early 1974 that there would be no new subsidies for highway construction, local support withered away, and only work connected with the metro station, including the demolition of several buildings, was actually undertaken. Planning continues, but with the aim, one city planning official told me, of allowing as little as possible to happen now so that more would be possible later.

One final project has begun in the Croix-Rousse along a street called the Grande Côte. Lyon's public works director described the project: "This is the worst housing in the city. It will be totally demolished to make way for open spaces. . . . This is about half an acre overpopulated with 600 or 700 people—mostly immigrant workers. It was a slum of no historic interest, built

Project	Plan fulfillment	Impact	Social change
Comprehensive Redevelopment I	high	high	low: low-income housing to low-income housing
Comprehensive Redevelopment II	high	high	low: low-income housing to low-income housing
Urban Renewal	medium	medium	low: low-income housing to low-income housing
Moncey Nord	medium	medium	high: low-income housing to costly housing
Part-Dieu	low	low	high: low-income housing and vacant land to costly housing and commercial center
Place Forez	medium	low	low: low-income housing to low-income housing
Martinière-Tolozan	low	medium	medium: low-income housing to costly housing
Grande Côte	low	low	high: low-income housing to parkland

around 1800, the neighborhood of the *canutes* [silk workers]. Certainly the most rundown neighborhood in the city. Buildings not in good condition, immigrants, many people per room." Although plans for the cleared site remained vague in mid-1975, the Grande Côte is noteworthy as the only site in Lyon acquired solely for the clearance of slum housing. The cleared site has been converted to parkland.

These eight projects in Lyon and Birmingham obviously vary in myriad ways. How do these differences reduce to the three measures developed in the preceding pages? The accompanying chart ranks each.

Several comments are in order. The second measure, "impact," requires a word about where projects could have been located, but were not. Unlike numerous American cities, neither Lyon nor Birmingham undertook its largest project in the central business district. In Lyon, such an approach was specifically rejected in favor of wholly new commercial construction at the Part-Dieu.[63] In Birmingham, developers did rebuild the city's principal railroad station as part of a large commercial complex, the Bull Ring. Further city-center renewal was proposed, but rejected.[64]

Several striking contrasts should be underscored. First, urban renewal in Lyon was not systematically directed at areas specifically defined by the state of physical decay; in Birmingham several thousand acres were treated as the city's worst housing, in Lyon, one half-acre. For this additional reason, I have assigned rather low ranking to the overall impact of Lyon's five projects. Second is the comparatively low level of control achieved over projects in Lyon: the city's efforts were consistently smaller and more changeable than were Birmingham's. Third, the projects' content differed greatly. A clear emphasis on eliminating slums and on providing subsidized, low-cost housing emerges for the Birmingham projects. Lyon's projects almost always produced costly housing and commercial space but did not have an important impact on the city's substandard housing. The bulk of Birmingham housing classified as unfit has simply been razed.

The differences are truly remarkable: Lyon and Birmingham were considerably more similar before urban renewal than after. Public authority and resources were in both cases powerful engines of change, but two different images of a revived city emerged from the working of these engines. What qualities, we may now ask, of government in the two cities led to these transformations and yet led them to be very different?

National Intervention and Urban Policy   2

What Kind of Centralization?

No modern state successfully escapes the need to delegate some of the responsibility and authority of government to subordinate territorial units. Whether rulers wish merely to maintain order and prevent secession or have grander aims of promoting justice and collective welfare, some method must be found to translate these goals into practice at points often far removed from the rulers' personal purview.

There are several reasons for this delegation. The first, writes Ivo Duchacek, "is simple enough: political rulers can focus on some problems some of the time but cannot focus on all problems all of the time in all localities."[1] Second, large modern nation-states tend to be diverse, encompassing widely varying economic, geographic, and social conditions. Attempts to implement nationwide measures must be tempered by sensitivity to varying local and regional conditions. By assigning some tasks to territorially dispersed government agencies, rulers can improve their ability to respond intelligently and accurately to these conditions. Third, citizens living away from a nation's center may demand that some decentralized authority, presumably more responsive to their wishes, be given jurisdiction over certain matters of public policy.

As a result not even the modern totalitarian state is governed exclusively from one capital.[2] Instead, countries develop a network of central government, its field offices, local and regional governments, and patterns by which these agencies deal with one another. For almost any important domestic policy issue, some combination of these national and subnational units will be called upon to act.[3] How such agencies go about cooperating, interfering, and competing will be an important determinant of what governments are in practice able to do.

However necessary it may be, delegation to subnational units produces a tension between the need to treat political problems uniformly throughout a polity and the pressure to respect heterogeneity and local wishes; between the virtues of centralizing as much power as possible and the virtues of locating a maximum of authority and responsibility near its point of application. Moreover, what looks like national domestic policy in the capital will no doubt look like urban policy from any other city. Which perspective should dominate decisions about any given issue is an open and a political question.[4]

While secession and civil war have resulted from extreme failures to resolve these tensions, no polity larger than a primitive village can entirely escape conflict between center and periphery. Countries that function with reasonable political stability have developed and institutionalized—often by force of arms—patterns for dividing the functions of government among various levels of authority. These patterns do not end the tensions; they do, however, provide a fairly stable and predictable institutional basis from which men and women responsible for a particular government can function in formulating and implementing public policy. The policies they successfully pursue must consequently reflect the incentives and constraints of these institutional arrangements. Thus the first element of political structure we must consider is the extent to which the French and British central governments dominate urban redevelopment programs in Lyon and Birmingham.

Centralization and Policy Control

France and Great Britain are both unitary states. In contrast to the situation in federal systems like the United States, territorial units are fundamentally the creation rather than the creators of the national states. Although these subnational units may enjoy powers reinforced by constitution and tradition, these powers remain in principle prerogatives of the central governments, amendable at the latter's command.

Implied within this characterization of the unitary state is considerable latitude for variation. If central authorities may delegate or retain specific powers, then we would expect that different governments in different times and places would develop differing patterns for the control and dispersal of both policy functions and the resources to carry out those functions. Powers, for example, may be delegated at one time and centralized at another; legal authority may reside at one level of government, requisite expertise and financial and political support at another; one central agency may closely supervise its provincial counterparts while another deals only with the most general questions of policy. The question we must then pose asks what difference these differing patterns may make for a policy issue like urban renewal.

We would expect urban renewal to be a policy issue that highlights central-local tensions. Urban renewal is the kind of activity that is simultaneously a local and a national policy issue. A program that attempts to redesign urban areas physically must profoundly affect the character, economy, and social environment of participating cities. The concern of local citizens and their leaders for the city's future is obvious. Viewed from the national capital, however, urban renewal appears as a component of various national domestic policy concerns, such as social welfare, economic development, and regional equalization. Thus a similar concern with the substance of any city's urban renewal program is also to be expected among national policymakers.

It should not be surprising, therefore, to find considerable tension between policymakers with essentially national concerns and constituencies and those with essentially local ones. While broad areas of cooperation between national and local authorities are sure to exist, the implementation of national policy goals for urban areas creates the grounds for considerable political conflict. The form and extent of this conflict, the substance and sequence of its occurrences are bound to affect the kinds of results any authority at any level actually achieves.

Out of a continuing concern with the complexities of federalism, numerous American scholars have considered ways in which such patterns of conflict and cooperation affect the results of policy efforts. A considerable body of scholarship argues that only in the presence of strong national intervention can urban policy goals be set and achieved in an efficient and equitable manner. E. E. Schattschneider, in a classic statement of this position, writes that when an issue is raised to a higher level of authority, for example, from a local to a national government, "a multitude of new resources for a resolution of conflict becomes available; solutions inconceivable at a lower level may be worked out at a higher level."[5] Schattschneider likens this elevation of conflict to the schoolyard situation in which small children faced by bullies run to "tell the teacher."[6]

The argument Schattschneider and others[7] make is double-edged. First of all, the national government is expected to deal more kindly with less privileged groups than lower levels of government. Or, in more general terms, the national government is more likely than local authorities to introduce broad social concerns into urban policymaking, to reduce the influence and independence of well-organized, narrow economic interest groups, and to increase attention to more general class issues.[8] In this view of central-local tension, the authority and objectivity of the national government are the key to effective policymaking.

Implicit within the central government as schoolteacher analogy is a second proposition. A country well endowed with institutional routes for central intervention in urban policymaking will, according to this analysis, more readily achieve long-term, difficult policy goals than a country less well endowed; the synoptic ideal will be more nearly realized in urban policymaking in more centralized countries. We would expect, therefore, that a higher level of policy control would be found in the country with central institutions most capable of intervention in local policymaking.

To examine this proposition, let us concentrate on bureaucracy, to which Sidney Tarrow refers as "the state's major concrete expression in the twentieth century"[9] and consider those agencies of the two central governments capable of taking on or directing urban renewal in Lyon and Birmingham and compare their abilities to intervene at the local level. We can then ask how well this comparison meshes with these expectations about levels of policy control. This investigation must, then, focus on each national government's network of field agencies and the relationships those agencies have developed with municipal authorities.

Lyon

The Prefecture

Considerable weight in tradition and scholarship supports the view that the degree of centralization in France is close to the limit of what is compatible with liberal democracy.[10] For those who hold this view, no institution symbolizes this centralization more clearly than does the prefect. Charged with maintaining civil order, promoting government policy, and representing the state's authority in each *département*,[11] the prefect, his subprefects, and his administrative entourage are usually considered the clear organizational reflection of French Jacobism, the dominance of the central state. The origins of this conception are not hard to find, as Howard Machin notes: "The Prefect is the head of the administration of a departement, and for this area he must fulfil the roles of lord lieutenant, emergency security commissioner, director general, chief constable, economic planning officer, local government supervisor, and executive officer for the departmental General Council. A reading of this astonishing list might lead one to believe that the Prefects are the omnipotent overlords of French provincial life."[12] Thus the provinces are conquered not only by division, but by the close scrutiny of a high-ranking civil servant with direct responsibilities to the central government stationed in each province's principal city.

The prefect is responsible for maintaining good order and furthering national policy in all parts of his *département*. The key element of his role in central-local relations, however, is the exercise of *la tutelle* (tutelage) over the villages, towns, and cities within his jurisdiction. An administrative law text describes this central feature of administrative control over local policymaking: *la tutelle* "is directed toward safeguarding the general interest, which is the state's charge, against the possible excesses of the decentralized authorities with respect to the legality and the general interest, and toward protecting the collectivity against the abuses of its administrators."[13] The image is clear: the representative of the state, and hence of the public interest, untrammeled by particular interests, is sent into the provinces to protect the citizenry against the narrow, self-seeking interests of local officials and to protect the nation from provincial rebellion. Thus the prefect is responsible for checking the legality of actions proposed by the municipal council, ensuring that local taxes are sufficient to provide obligatory services and a balanced budget, and approving each grant of government money to be used locally.[14] These powers sound extensive, and for most of France's 37,000 communes, they are probably sufficient to smother any gasps of municipal self-assertion.

Such a view is, however, inadequate for several reasons. First of all, preventing abuses may have been a reasonable approach to managing urban problems before the rapid and accelerating movement to French cities that followed World War II; it surely was inadequate thereafter. Problems arose that demanded attention, and purposeful initiatives became crucial regardless of source. Second, *la tutelle* may have been possible and appropriate for the small, rural communes whose aversion to collective action is picturesquely displayed in studies like those of Mark Kesselman or Laurence Wylie,[15] but ensuring legality and the fulfillment of statutory services is hardly a basis for taking an active part in the political issues of large, heterogeneous cities like Lyon. Furthermore, because the prefecture is largely staffed by legal experts, it is itself dependent upon other ministerial services for technical assistance. Prefecture officials with whom I spoke referred to reports prepared in technical agencies as the bases for their judgments and decisions. And finally, there is no reason to believe that the prefect and the minister of the interior for whom he works will be any less susceptible to the pressures of political factions than anyone else, or that the pressures of this sort will not come from the administered city. In other words, the prefect cannot depend on his formal authority to defend his position in the face of determined opposition from other well-connected actors in the local political arena. This last point is particularly important and requires some explanation.

First the prefect may not be the only major central government figure in his *département*. Except for his internment during part of the Vichy regime, Edouard Herriot was mayor of Lyon from 1905 until his death in 1957. During that time he was also president of the Council of Ministers (prime minister) on several occasions and presided over the Third Republic's Chamber of Deputies and the Fourth Republic's National Assembly.[16] Jacques Chelban-Delmas occupied the mayor's suite in Bordeaux's city hall before, during, and after his stay at Matignon. Both Georges Pompidou and Valéry Giscard d'Estaing were at once president of the Republic and village mayor. The examples can easily be multiplied: nearly half the cabinet appointed after the 1978 National Assembly elections were mayors, but the point is that the prefect, like any official with the authority to give or withhold desirable public favors, finds himself in a complex political network working with mayors, deputies, ministers, and even heads of state.

As Jean-Claude Thoenig makes clear, this network does not require a Giscard to be an effective limit on prefectural action: "The prefect and the principal heads of departmental administrative services find themselves under the control of the local political milieu, and in particular of the most important officials like senators and deputies. They [local politicians] have direct access to Paris and entreé into ministerial cabinets. In their *département* they have the influence to mobilize behind them persons with political, social, and economic responsibilities. The prefect, the departmental directors for Equipement or Social Welfare depend for their career upon the fact that in their *département* matters are taken care of quickly and without arousing the hostility of local elites."[17]

In other words, the ability of the prefect to interfere in local matters, should he judge it necessary, is severely limited by the influence and connections of local politicians. A Provençal mayor nicely illustrated Thoenig's argument when he told Tarrow, "We have good relations with the subprefect, but we frequently short-circuit them because we have good contacts in Paris."[18] Even in Lyon, where Louis Pradel, mayor during most of the urban renewal program, held no higher office, officials in the prefecture explained to me their reluctance to block an objectionable public works project by saying "M. Pradel is someone: when he telephones, the minister answers." Moreover, as Thoenig implies, the prefect must act to protect his career by avoiding "*des histoires*"[19] and by having accomplishments to point to, objectives that local opposition can hinder.

Thus objecting in the "general interest" to local initiatives that local leaders favor is unlikely to occupy much of the prefect's time. Surely his role is more often that of negotiator or advocate than guardian. Pierre Grémion and Jean-Pierre Worms conclude from their studies of several prefectures that "there is less conflict than profound complicity between the field services of the state and local political officials."[20]

This argument does not imply that ministry officials assigned to prefectures in provincial France are mere figureheads, reluctant to take controversial positions and unsupported by their superiors. The importance of stationing ninety-five high, elite-corps civil servants in towns and cities throughout the country lies more in the ability of the prefect and his associates to promote the political fortunes of the government and to provide information and intelligence to both Paris and the *département*, than in any ongoing role the prefect may have in determining the substance of major policy issues like urban renewal.

Furthermore, the policy implications of the prefect's political role cannot be ignored. French mayors in Tarrow's sample did contact other central government field officers more often than the prefect, but they also sought out the prefect for "special favors."[21] Similarly, central and local government officials who were directly concerned with planning and executing urban renewal projects frequently told me of the prefecture's attention to the details of a specific project. The prefect, without commenting on general design or programmatic matters, often adjusted the balance of projects among municipalities in the Lyonnais region or requested that deviations from plans be made for specific individuals or groups. The prefect thus retained significant responsibilities for the distribution of the inevitable favors urban renewal could provide. Such actions are on the one hand the kind of compromises that are frequently needed to ensure support for major policy ventures, and on the other hand the first indication that central intervention is not necessarily consistent with the synoptic ideal.

Technical Field Offices: The DDE and the SCET

If accepted views of French policymaking as a highly centralized process now appear somewhat questionable, part of the reason lies in the tendency of this traditional view and its critiques to overemphasize the role of the prefecture as the vehicle of this centralization. Central intervention in French urban policy is considerable; we must look at other institutions, however, for a more accurate view of both its means and its policy implications.

I noted above that the prefecture depends upon other central government agencies for technical advice in matters like the evaluation of municipal initiatives and requests for grants. The planners and engineers in these offices provide the central government's chief mode of intervention in the planning and execution of major urban policy efforts. Although field officials of these technical agencies are the legal subordinates of the prefect—they must, for example, address all reports and recommendations to the prefect—the nature of the experts' work places them in an influential and independent position with regard both to the prefect and to the local government. Not only do technical officials enjoy the usual advantage of the specialist confronting the generalist, but their careers are more dependent on their own ministry and service corps than on the goodwill of the prefect.[22] To understand the contributions of these agencies to urban redevelopment in Lyon, we need to trace central intervention along two rather complex organizational paths.

Until the 1960s the preeminent reservoir for the technical and administrative skills needed for public works projects throughout France resided in the variously named construction and public works ministries. Reinforcing the centralist structure of the prefectures, these ministries staffed large departmental offices (called the Directions départementales) with members of the civil service corps of Travaux publics and, more important, the elite Corps des Ponts et chaussées. The last, whose name means Bridges and Roadways Corps, Ezra Suleiman has likened to the United States Army Corps of Engineers: highly skilled in both engineering and politics and thus highly independent in policy-making.[23] This combination of political and technical weight made the Direction départementale du Rhône of the amalgamated Ministère de l'Equipement[24] (the DDE) the first central government agency to have a direct and systematic role in the development of Lyon's urban renewal policies.

The technical basis for the DDE's importance results from the public works corps' long-time monopoly on France's civil engineering talent. Since its creation under the ancien régime, the Corps des Ponts has not only carried out major provincial public works projects, but has even supplied departmental councils and municipalities with the major part of their technical staffing.

Lyon was no exception to this dependence. Before the city established its own city planning department in 1962, it depended completely upon DDE planners to develop local land-use policy. In fact the land-use and housing studies that identified sectors of Lyon ripe for urban renewal were carried out in the mid- and late 1950s by field officers of the Ministère de la Reconstruction et du logement, the Ministère de l'Equipement's precursor.[25] The renewal projects actually undertaken and the projects that local officials still consider future possibilities are in sectors of the city identified by these studies.

Even after the city had established its own independent technical services, the DDE engineers and planners continued to provide local officials with detailed technical advice about Lyon's projects.[26] When I asked a DDE engineer with administrative responsibilities to comment on overlap between municipal and Direction responsibilities, he stressed that the technical agencies were "not parallel, but competitive." They were mutually "interventionist." Frequency of contact between Direction and municipal officials was apparent from informants' references to these contacts and from the regularity with which my conversations with officials of one agency were interrupted by telephone calls from officials employed at another level of government. Subjects of these observed and reported conversations included quite fundamental topics such as the amount of low-income housing to include in an already operational project as well as more prosaic matters like the design of roadways.

Municipal officials look to DDE engineers and planners for reasons beyond their skill and experience. Subsidies for public works require the prefect's signature; if enough money or disruption is involved (as in urban renewal, for example) the minister of équipement must concur. Who prepares the report advising the prefect or minister on his decision? The Direction départementale de l'Equipement. The advisability of engaging the Direction in preparing the project is clear.

Moreover, the ministry offices and the engineering corps are important channels of communication for local and national officials. Because he has frequent personal contacts with government employees, the technical field officer is an important conduit for the complaints, appeals, and advice that are the daily substance of intergovernmental relations. In distinct contrast to what we find in Great Britain, these administrative contacts are the most important channels of intergovernmental contact even when party links local and national officials.[27]

The Direction provides a significant central presence in the planning and execution of urban renewal projects, but once again the operative word is Grémion and Worms's: "complicity." Engineers who work for the Direction perform their work in accordance with governmental positions on urban development issues. On the other hand, as one official admitted, "We defend the [local] collectivity vis-à-vis the central powers. We're halfway between the point of view of the minister and that of the locals. Our preoccupation is local; we have common interests." He expressed a similar ambivalence at another point in our discussion: "We must pay attention to the point of view of the minister. . . . An example of policy at this level is the reduction in growth of the large cities. This is government policy, but the mayor does not necessarily agree." Here is a man who clearly considers himself a hybrid, at once the representative of the central and the local government.

Like many of his colleagues this engineer followed a career pattern that reinforced his dual identification. His thirty years in Lyon are typical of all but the very top DDE officials, who spend at most five years at any one assignment. The majority of officials, after training and a stint in Paris, make their careers in a provincial office and develop the identifications and concerns of a local citizen.[28]

In short the Direction provided two important links in organizational relations. First, as a technical conduit, it directed personnel with professional and training links to Paris into the thick of decision making for local projects. Second, as a political conduit, it brought together the interests and aims of both local and central policymakers and thereby provided a means for negotiation between them. It is not, therefore, important to decide whether the Direction was an instrument of central control or the co-opted ally of local leaders. What is important to recognize is the agency's strategically powerful position that both made D D E officials regular participants in the planning and execution of urban renewal in Lyon and facilitated local influence on the way in which national urban policy would be carried out.

Consideration of the technical arms of the central government makes central intervention seem more important for the substantive issues of urban renewal than attention to the prefectural network alone. The patterns of central-local interaction are, however, still more complex.

Despite their considerable presence in designing and implementing urban development and redevelopment schemes, the technical ministries are not without organizational rivals. François d'Arcy and Bruno Jobert have considered the relative positions in the early 1960s of those central agencies concerned with urban planning: "At the administrative and political level the Ministry of . . . Housing was the most important body, the local authorities still playing only a small role. But it was a weak ministry, over-centralized, its personnel being of high average age and of rather low average quality. In the case of operational town planning, it let itself be relieved of a part of its prerogatives by a body created by the *Caisse des Dépôts et consignations* [a public bank][29] peripheral to the official administrative services: the Central Office for Territorial Investment [Société centrale pour l'Equipement du territoire or the S C E T]."[30]

Although the Ministère de la Construction et du logement, to which d'Arcy and Jobert refer, has been reorganized out of existence, the S C E T retains a major role in urban renewal. To see how it does this, we must consider still another breed of organizational participant in urban renewal.

Owing to the complexities of administrative law, French municipalities have great legal difficulties in negotiating the purchase and sale of land and acquiring the capital necessary for public projects like urban renewal; they also find it difficult to offer salaries sufficient to attract into their employ persons capable of these negotiations. As a result, municipalities and *dépar-*

tements have established sociétés d'économie mixte (SEMs, or mixed corporations) to undertake the implementation of major urban development projects such as large peripheral developments (the *grands ensembles*), new towns, and urban renewal projects.[31] In Lyon the Société d'Equipement de la région lyonnaise (SERL) has filled this role.

These corporations enjoy all the financial and judicial freedom of private firms, but remain, in conception at least, the tools of the local authorities that create them and own the majority of their stock. That conception is imperfectly borne out, however, because of the close ties between each corporation and the central administration, ties that pass through the SCET.

The SCET, like the development corporations, was created in an attempt to circumvent normal administrative channels and expedite action in urban development. In fact, according to d'Arcy, the minister of finance arranged in 1955 for the Caisse des Dépôts to create and finance the SCET expressly so that the local development corporations could be expeditiously supplied with both finances and expertise: "The local administration lacked the means to fill this role. As for the state administration, it was too divided and not always desirous of plunging into new experiments."[32] Both because of its financial resources and because of its relatively unencumbered operational style, the SCET quickly became an important means of governmental action in urban development. Accordingly, the ministries concerned with municipal administration, the finance ministry, and the interministerial committee on regional development have all been active participants in the management of the SCET.[33] And because the SCET has remained quite centralized in its own operation, this arrangement has allowed these government officials a direct means to affect the planning and operation of local development projects.

The SCET maintains this influence because it plays a key role in the operation of the development corporations and because the corporations play an equally key role in urban development projects. The SCET's ability to provide its corporations with interim financing—primarily for land acquisition—makes the commencement of urban renewal projects possible. In Lyon this financial strength could be and was used as leverage to promote certain kinds of developments and discourage others.

Again the argument here is not that the SCET and the Direction took over urban renewal in Lyon; the importance of strictly local institutions will become increasingly clear. The point is rather that through these groups of organizations, authorities with national constituencies and responsibilities had direct means for affecting the substance of urban renewal projects in Lyon.

Two points stand out: first, three substantially independent organizational paths led from Paris directly to decisions about urban redevelopment in Lyon. Second, each of these paths terminated in field organizations with the political and in two cases the independent technical ability to participate actively in initiating, developing, and executing urban renewal programs. As a result, central government officials intervened, not just as advance planners nor simply as guardians of national subsidies, but as active participants in policymaking and execution throughout a project's life: advance planning, site selection, acquisition, clearance, disposal, and reconstruction.

Political Parties and Centralization

French political parties do not play a major part in a discussion of the role of central-local political relationships in urban renewal. Something similar will be the case for Britain. This emphasis is in keeping with an analytic framework that uses organizations to represent institutionalized patterns of political resources and political relationships; in Fifth Republic France, political parties do not provide the organizational base for any political relationship crucial to urban renewal. While Lyon may be the extreme case—mayors during most of the period under consideration ostentatiously eschewed party labels for themselves and their city council coalitions—weak adherence to national parties (excepting always the Communists) has been found generally among leaders of French municipalities.[34]

Most important, the irrelevance of party ties underscores the emphasis given above to relationships within and among administrative organizations. Three important results follow from the use of administrative agencies as the channel of communication between Paris and provincial cities. First, this channel is open to municipal officials regardless of party.[35] Second, the administration directs both to and from Paris requests, information, and objections bearing on issues of varying content. Third, as a result of the first two conditions, the issue in any matter of dispute becomes blurred; authentic technical problems, favors for political supporters, and major policy disputes are dealt with simultaneously and as administrative matters, matters to be resolved as specific decisions must be made.

This last point, in fact, summarizes the character of structured relationships between local and central authorities in France. A plurality of central agencies intervenes directly and thereby affects the course of urban policymaking. The pattern of central-local relations provides for different kinds of intervention—technical criticism, particularistic favoritism, financial restraint, broad social questioning—continuously throughout the design and implementation of a project and brings a variety of perspectives—partisan, technical, administrative, financial—to bear on the myriad decisions involved in the realization of urban renewal programs.

Central Intervention and Urban Development

The parallel evolution of national urban policy and Lyon's urban renewal effort shows the impact of these multiple courses of central intervention. An official of the Ministère de l'Equipement central office in Paris described the course of national perspectives on urban redevelopment over fifteen years: "In 1958, we thought of slums, and it was a national priority to get rid of them. In 1962 with the *Loi Malraux*, we said that we demol-

ished too much and should preserve the interesting neighborhoods—only the interesting ones. Then came the idea of regional development and restoration and the sixth plan and the
métropoles d'équilibre, and specific kinds of projects were fa-
vored. Now we try to conserve more, not just the historically interesting." Described here are at least four major shifts in national urban renewal policy made over a comparatively short
period. In different ways these shifts were reflected on the
ground in Lyon.

Because the various central agencies that developed these approaches to urban renewal were linked directly to policymaking
at the local level, these national-level shifts in perspective on urban renewal were directly translated into projects or aspects of
projects in Lyon. Because, however, these linkages were multiple and varied, the translations were complex and imperfect.

The official decree providing municipalities with powers to
carry out urban renewal was issued at the end of 1958, but the
urban planning group for the Lyon region of the Ministère de la
Reconstruction et du logement had already begun identifying
sectors and setting priorities for redevelopment of the city's
older neighborhoods. According to the ministry plan, earliest
efforts would be made in the left-bank area followed by preservation work in the city's Renaissance quarter and redevelopment
of the Croix-Rousse.[36]

The city would first capitalize on the site acquired in the
Moncey Nord sector and then move on to the more extensive
Part-Dieu project. According to the director of the DDE planning office, who in the mid-1950s was a planner with that agency,
ministry planners were especially anxious to interest the city in
adopting the Part-Dieu project and were instrumental in making
arrangements for the transfer of the property from the army.
"No one believed us," he said. "An important local industrialist
told me, 'You'll never sell one single square meter.' Pradel [mayor
of Lyon, elected in 1957] wouldn't believe us. It was up to the
state to organize things. It was the Ministère de la Construction
that pushed the project." The start of urban renewal in Lyon de-

pended not only upon the ministry's technical and planning resources, but also upon its ability to work closely with central and
local officials and to push programs at both levels.

Thus, in early 1960, under pressure from the construction
ministry and its Lyon field offices, the Lyon municipal council
undertook its first urban renewal projects at Moncey Nord and
the Part-Dieu.[37] Significantly, the initial ministry push was limited to these two projects on the left bank of the Rhone. Projects
in other sectors that were included in the Direction report did
not begin for another decade at least. Central intervention did
not, however, end with these initial prods to action. Further
pressures would change profoundly the substance of the projects.

Before land cession at the Part-Dieu was complete and before
construction at Moncey Nord had begun, France embarked upon
an ambitious and multifaceted program of regional economic
and cultural development.[38] The redevelopment of older provincial cities became a major component of this program. When urban renewal began to change from a slum clearance program to a
means for regional development, agencies tied to Paris were
once again instrumental in redirecting local policy in Lyon.

Guiding the regional development program from its inception
was the concern that Paris had become an overgrown monster,
environmentally inhospitable, logistically impossible, and politically dangerous, while the rest of the country—*la territoire*—
increasingly resembled a cultural and economic desert.[39] Along
with offering subsidies to firms investing outside greater Paris,
promoting new towns, and increasing investment in provincial
public facilities and industrial infrastructure, the government in
1968 designated Lyon and seven other provincial cities as *métropoles d'équilibre*, urban centers that could grow and offset the
overstrong attractions to capital and labor that Paris continued
to provide.[40] "A corrective policy," one of its originators and promoters wrote, "was thus put into operation aimed at limiting the
Paris region's growth and at promoting the large metropolitan
areas so that they could receive the overflow from the Paris region."[41] This effort at promotion would, according to Monod, di-

rect the whole range of public investments in the *métropoles* and would in particular lead to an emphasis on transportation, urban development, industrial development, and expansion of the tertiary sector. This emphasis is underscored by the relative neglect of towns with declining industry or agriculture that had little prospect of becoming business service centers. [42]

Support for regional development programs came from the highest levels of the French government. Of particular importance for Lyon and the Part-Dieu was the interest of François Bloch-Lainé in the development of the large provincial cities. Even before the official promulgation of the *métropole d'équilibre* program, of which he was an author, Bloch-Lainé used his successive directorships of the SCET and the Caisse des Dépôts to promote tertiary growth in cities like Lyon. With financial and technical support from the SCET, Marseille, Bordeaux, and Rennes all committed themselves in the mid-1960s to the production of large, modern commercial and business centers. The Part-Dieu was Lyon's contribution to this effort. [43]

In a political process that can be traced back through the second path of central intervention in urban policymaking the Part-Dieu became the symbol of Lyon's new image as *métropole d'équilibre*. As with most major, publicly directed construction projects in and around Lyon, the municipal council delegated administration of the Part-Dieu project to the SERL. That corporation would, on the city's behalf, manage purchases from the army and from owners of the surrounding land to be included in the project, clearance of the land, and eventual sales to builders and developers. Following current ministerial and municipal policy, the SERL then launched the project. A group of architects prepared a residential plan for the redevelopment of the cleared land, and contracts were let for the construction of an initial group of apartment buildings on the first parcel of land the army had ceded.

The city's agreements with the army, however, transferred ownership of the Part-Dieu gradually, over nearly a decade. Between the city's acquisition of this first parcel and additional cessions, the national regional development policy gained momentum. The SCET, which was providing both technical and financial support for the Part-Dieu project, began to supply the SERL with architects and city planners sympathetic to tertiary sector development schemes. By 1965 the SERL, in collaboration with the newly established municipal urban planning office, announced a wholly revised project.[44] Instead of housing, the Part-Dieu would provide Lyon with a new central business district and greatly expanded commercial, office, and hotel facilities. At the same time the Moncey Nord project was reduced to those portions of the original project that directly abutted the Part-Dieu project; other plans for the sector were dropped.[45]

Central intervention was not, however, limited to massive projects like the Part-Dieu. Collaboration between central and local officials followed other changes in national redevelopment policy. The Place Forez project is an illustrative case.

In both France and Great Britain (and in the United States) urban renewal began with the wholesale clearance of slum neighborhoods. The social and financial costs[46] of clearance projects, however, led to considerable controversy and to the search for less costly and less disruptive alternatives. By the mid-1960s, again in both countries, strategies had emerged for combining preservation with planned revival.[47]

As one Lyonnais planner described the matter, "Redevelopment ran up against structures that were too resistant and communities that were also too resistant." The alternative strategies, as a consequence, aimed at projects that left intact the physical and social outlines of existing neighborhoods. Wherever possible, buildings would be repaired, refurbished, and equipped with modern conveniences, although extreme deterioration or plans for neighborhood facilities—parking, parks, widened streets—would lead to occasional selective demolition. The alternative made fiscal, social, and political sense; it even could fit the idea of planned urban change. The problem was how to introduce the innovation. In Lyon the solution was clear.

Ministerial study groups working in Paris developed the outlines for plans to introduce preservation and restoration into French urban renewal programs.[48] In contrast, however, to what we shall see in Birmingham, the network of organizational links between central agencies and local policymaking provided direct means to activate such programs at the local level. According to the ARIM director in Lyon, the Ministère de la Construction simply set up voluntary organizations like his own in each of the fifteen cities in which projects were to be attempted. The DDE orchestrated agreements among local architects, housing officials, builders, and other ministry officials to create a local, non-profit housing rehabilitation organization. This organization would work with the municipal governments to design and implement pilot projects.

The ministry then financed the ARIM's planning and architectural work; the Directions départementales provided technical support and supervision. Specific proposals, however, required municipal approval, and any orders for compulsory repairs had to come from the city. In other words, the central government could introduce the new strategy, but its realization required joint action by local and central authorities. As we shall see, it soon became clear in Lyon that the city administration was unwilling to shoulder the political and financial burden that the use of its expropriation powers would have imposed. Central intervention was sufficient to initiate the project, but the municipal support needed to carry it out was not forthcoming.

The reverse of this pattern is apparent in the Martinière-Tolozan project. In this case the withdrawal of central intervention, in the form of an expressway grant, stopped the project. Lacking national support, municipal officials could only tread the urban planning water and avoid foreclosure of alternatives for the renewal of the sector.

If relations between central and local governments ever resembled a marble cake,[49] France surely offers a prominent example of such a confection. Not only does the central government retain the technical and financial resources to intervene in urban policymaking, it distributes that capacity to intervene over the course of a given program. Central agencies may participate in early planning studies, in the technical problems of preparing a specific project, or in the fine details of implementation. And yet in each case that participation is dependent, as we shall see, on the cooperation of local politicians, administrators, and interest groups as well. The marble cake is still further complicated because "central intervention" itself comes in several different flavors, all mixed or separated in varying degrees. Comparison with Great Britain demonstrates the importance of this complexity for the substance of policy matters.

Birmingham

Technical Field Offices

Much as a cursory view of the legal arrangements for French field administration leaves the impression of considerable central control, so British cities appear on the surface to carry out urban policy quite autonomously. In practice, once again, the relationships are much more complex and such characterizations misleading. More important, a closer look shows that attempts to sum up the policy of central intervention in urban policy with one measure of centralization is not a helpful approach to comparing public policy among nations.

In part Britain looks less centralized than France because the large, technically oriented outposts of field administration that play a major role in French urban politics simply are not found in Great Britain. This contrast reflects not merely staffing decisions, but rather quite different structures of administrative organization.

According to two British students of French public administration, F. F. Ridley and Jean Blondel, "While British ministries are fairly compact organizations located almost wholly in London, French ministries have a wide network of regional and local branches and a multitude of functional agencies."[50] This contrast, argues L. James Sharpe, results from a differing view of the role of the central government in domestic policy. Except for the National Health Service and social welfare, "British central government does not concern itself directly with executant activities. Central government confines itself to the roles of policy making, of regulation, of inspecting, of guiding, advising and controlling and in the main leaves operational responsibilities to an executant agency" (the principal ones being local government, the public corporations, and "quasi-non-governmental" organizations).[51] Does this "non-executant tradition"[52] leave no role for central intervention in urban revival programs?

The important role the Department of the Environment and its previously separate section, the Ministry of Housing and Local Government,[53] play in urban renewal policy reveals that a considerable national role remains. "The Ministry," wrote its long-time permanent secretary (the highest civil service official) Dame Evelyn Sharp, "is, very largely, a headquarters department."[54] Ministry officials do not usually have a direct role in shaping the details of urban programs. She continues: "In a great deal of its work the Ministry's statutory role is largely negative. It is the local authorities which are expected to take the initiative."[55] "Almost everything which Ministers seek to achieve, apart from the building of new towns, must be done by the local authorities."[56] As we shall see, "nonexecutant" does not mean "noninterventionist," but the organizational contrast with French field administration is clear.[57]

The central government's dependence on local authorities for the realization of policy is reflected in the structure of its agencies and organizations. In contrast to the Directions and the regional offices of the SCET, the Department of the Environment simply does not employ sufficient technical specialists to assume an active role in the development and implementation of major urban development schemes. J. A. G. Griffith, writing at what was about the mid-course point of Birmingham's redevelopment program, reports that the small size of the department's staff (about sixty-four architects and twenty-three quantity surveyors[58] for all housing purposes) limits the policy role the department can play. Ministry officials consequently may not see local housing plans until they have been approved by the city council and even bid on. At this point, any attempt to affect policy would cause significant delay. Indeed, ministry officials play a role in developing projects for smaller towns,[59] but an active interventionist role simply is not built into the relationship between the ministry field offices and the administration of large cities like Birmingham.

I asked a quantity surveyor in the West Midlands regional office of the Department of the Environment (located in Birmingham) if he was a source of technical advice for city officials planning renewal projects. He replied that a city as large and "powerful" as Birmingham would never turn to ministry personnel for technical advice. "They've more architects and quantity surveyors than the whole of the department. If they asked us for advice, we'd find it laughable." Regional officials are a significant presence in Birmingham, especially in monitoring local compliance with national policy. Compared to French field officers, however, they were less interventionist. Direction engineers were in constant consultation with local officials about the substance of Lyon's urban renewal projects; their British counterparts did not consider that kind of participation part of their jobs.

Whatever means for exerting central control over urban renewal may exist in Great Britain, a route through ministry officials who work directly on the substance of projects does not exist. The regional director, the Department of the Environment undersecretary in charge of the West Midlands regional office, explains: as a representative of the central government, he "can stop an authority from doing something, but we can't force them to build. . . . Birmingham sets up its housing policy: what they build, whom for—old, young families—what they tear down, what balance of new buildings." Two points emerge: first, central control in Britain differs from that found in France; second, such control does exist.

Legal and Financial Control

The regional director's claim to authority to block local action is based on his authority to refuse applications for subsidies, to refuse to approve orders for compulsory land sales to the local authority, and to refuse permission for the local authority to borrow heavily enough to finance a project. Each of these powers is available to delegates of the French government, but the contrasting manner in which they are employed highlights the crucial difference between French and British local-national political relations.

Lacking the technical personnel to participate in the evaluation of local problems and in the planning for their amelioration, the ministry lacks the capacity to contribute actively to the development of local urban renewal projects. What these central officials can do is evaluate local proposals against nationally ordained project standards and criteria[60] and, through the regional offices, monitor the results of projects. National government policies impose uniform structural and amenity standards for municipal housing construction, uniform definitions for unfit housing, and uniform criteria for subsidies and loan approvals.[61] These project requirements do not serve simply to prevent shoddy construction, capricious expropriations, irresponsible financial management, or gross regional inequities,[62] but, in fact, greatly constrain local choices about the substance of policies. For example, the heavy Exchequer subsidies available for the construction and operation of municipal housing made any other use of the land cities acquired from slum clearance projects fiscally unfeasible.[63]

Central intervention, in short, takes a different course in Britain than in France. Deciding whether a given project does or does not meet stated requirements for structural quality or for fiscal soundness is quite a different matter from deciding whether in specific cases urban renewal should first be in the worst or in the most rapidly decaying part of the city or whether redevelopment should emphasize residential or commercial construction. Whereas French central authorities were heavily involved in decisions of the latter sort, British ministerial officials were chiefly involved with the former for Birmingham.

The account of administrative differences, thus, does not imply that France is in some summary sense the more centralized country. Strict regulation rigorously applied is an effective means of central intervention even if municipalities carry out redevelopment projects alone. Moreover British central intervention is enhanced relative to French by the way it is applied. The central-local complicity I emphasized in discussing French field administration does play a comparable decentralizing role in Britain. Ashford goes so far as to say that "the complex interaction of mayors, local and central officials, and national politicians so common in France is unknown in Britain. The result is that in functional terms the dominance of the Whitehall cadre over local affairs may be much greater than that of the French bureaucracy. In this respect Britain is more centralized than France."[64] Leaving aside the question of which country is more centralized, without the French network of complicity to soften their impact, legal and financial controls make British cities less autonomous than administrative structures alone would imply.

Accordingly, ministry inspectors and engineers will make sure that houses to be cleared have the requisite number of structural flaws and that redevelopment plans meet quality and cost standards, and ministers and higher civil servants will make sure that the government's social service and public investment aims are upheld, but each will respect the municipal government's authority to design and execute whatever plans those standards permit. Thus, for example, every large British industrial city has since World War II cleared large areas of slum housing and has built municipal low-income housing on the cleared land, but from preliminary studies through the selection of priority areas through the design and execution of individual projects, work has been carried out independently by officials of each municipal authority. This independence had led to substantial local variation.[65]

Political Parties and Central Intervention

Fesler warns that partisan factors might significantly alter the balance of influence between central and local officials, however their jobs may in principle be constituted.[66] In a fashion not found in France, British political parties lay an organization network over British politics that might be expected to affect the relationship between central and local authorities. City council leaders in virtually every British city adhere to one of the major national parties and fight municipal elections and city council debates under party colors. Two possible results for the resolution of local policy matters warrant more attention to British parties in this context than was paid in France. First, the national parties could discipline their municipal followers, as members of Parliament are disciplined, to ensure that Whitehall-conceived policy was assiduously applied when the national party formed the government and similarly resisted when the national party was in opposition. Second, the national party organization might, as Fesler argues, be a vehicle for resistance in London to requirements or restrictions placed on local authorities in the provinces. The stronger, more nationally integrated parties might play the role personal and bureaucratic networks played in France.[67]

Do the British national parties impose a party line, a prescribed, uniform course of action, on members active in municipal politics? The best answer is that they do not, but for the most part they do not need to. Austin Ranney's conclusions about party control over local party organizations' selection of parliamentary candidates are comparable and instructive. Ranney found virtually no evidence suggesting that the central party organizations could dictate choices, but he did find that "the local parties voluntarily continue to adopt candidates who, when elected, dutifully vote as the whips [in Parliament] suggest."[68]

In a similar fashion, local party organizations usually adopt positions on local issues that mesh with national party policy. [69] When, for example, Birmingham Conservatives took office in 1966, they immediately and ostentatiously began trying to sell municipally owned houses to current tenants. When the Labour Party regained city council control in 1972, its leaders acted quickly to stop such sales. [70] Birmingham Tories dragged their feet on moving to establish comprehensive schools; their Labour successors moved more expeditiously. [71] As George Jones argues, local and national politics are often "two skirmishes . . . of one battle fought by the same armies." [72] National organizations normally do not seek to control municipal politicians because a common set of objectives and a common constituency provide sufficient uniformity.

Discord is, however, inevitable. When it occurs in matters of municipal policymaking, central party organizations lack even the powers they hold in the candidate selection process. [73] John Gyford writes, "It is apparent that both in the Labour and Conservative Parties there are neither the constitutional mechanisms, nor the resources, nor the inclination to permit the effective central control of the parties' local councillors." [74] Birmingham leaders of both the Conservative and the Labour parties discounted policy pressure from Smith Square, and officials responsible for local government in both parties' central offices denied exercising effective control, especially over the largest authorities like Birmingham.

The national party offices do, on the other hand, serve as a liaison between local and national politicians for information or complaints on specific policy issues. [75] Furthermore, the impact on a local politician of a telephone call from a minister or shadow minister cannot be doubted. Thus, while local leaders could and did violate party positions in city council actions without fear of serious reprisal, [76] the national political parties do provide a link in the pattern of intervention considered above. This point requires elaboration.

Commentators have frequently connected weak party organi-

zations to the weak position of the American federal government
in the resolution of urban policy issues. Theodore Lowi, for example, argues that the decentralized American party system inhibits central intervention by permitting local party barons to
demand exceptions to unwelcome federal rulings.[77] The British
system of centralization by regulation assumes that this kind of
partisan erosion will not occur. To the extent that Lowi's argument holds, however, the strength of parliamentary and party
headquarters organizations should make British ministries less
susceptible to local pressures. In fact it does just that. Ashford
argues that "Britain has been able to control territorial politics
because the direct intervention of local partisan interests and
parties in national government is for the most part cut off . . .
the absence of strong territorial politics in Britain contrasts
sharply with the French system and may well be linked to parliamentary stability and power."[78] The political parties provide a
means of communication and of pressure without generating the
complex networks of influence found in France or the United
States. Communication through party channels has a distinctly
legislative quality: What do rules mean? How will they be applied? In what ways should they be changed? But rarely: Can we
get around them? I found no point at which party-motivated exceptions to established government policy substantially affected
the course of urban renewal in Birmingham.[79] Parties, in short,
reinforce the legal and financial patterns of central intervention
in Britain.

A marble cake of complex interdependency and overlap systematically characterized relations between Lyon and Paris. Just
as consistently a contrasting pattern of clearly separate layers
characterized central-local relations in Britain. Birmingham's relationship with governmental agencies was based upon general
rules and categories set in London by national authorities but
applied in Birmingham by local ones, the relationship proceeded
by adjudication and arbitration, and it insulated the broadest
policy questions from their application. Stanley Hoffman has
written of the meshing of rulemaking and rule enforcement in

the hands of the French national executive,[80] while L. J. Sharpe has argued that "nowhere in the Western World is the line [between politics and administration] less blurred than in Britain."[81] Within the framework of central dominance, Birmingham's urban renewal programs demonstrated the continued separation of these two functions. The consequences of this separation are especially clear in the context of changes in similar directions of urban renewal policy in Birmingham and Lyon.

Central Intervention and Urban Renewal

The launching of Birmingham's Comprehensive Redevelopment Program stands the Part-Dieu story almost exactly on its head. As Birmingham's chief engineer, Herbert Manzoni began developing schemes to redevelop central Birmingham under the rather constraining provisions of pre–World War II housing and town-planning legislation.[82] The restraints on civilian investment that Britain's military effort engendered interrupted these plans but also provided an opportunity to refine and expand them. The interregnum also permitted a ministry committee of which Manzoni was one of three members to review national urban development legislation. From that committee's deliberations grew the 1944 Town and Country Planning Act under which Birmingham expeditiously acquired ownership of the 1,100 acres that were to become the first five Redevelopment Areas.[83]

This series of events is not an indication that local authorities design national legislation to suit local purposes. Rather the parallel development of the 1944 act and Birmingham's Comprehensive Redevelopment Program illustrates the highly legislative, rule-making focus of local-national relations in Great Britain.

Even when a major change in urban renewal strategy originated in London, implementation remained a separate, locally controlled matter. This separation was clearly revealed when the central government began, at about the same time as in France, to introduce and promote preservation and rehabilitation as major elements in urban renewal programs. The goals and strategies were strikingly similar in the two countries; the political and administrative methods for introducing changes were not.[84]

The revised British strategy was first announced systematically in a 1968 White Paper entitled "Old Houses into New Homes" and then built into the Housing Act of 1969. In light of the preceding discussion, the means adopted for implementing the change are no surprise. The 1969 act, as one Department of the Environment official told me, "made it more or less equally attractive to build [new municipal housing] or to improve [existing private housing]. It had been more attractive to clear and rebuild." The 1969 act and successive refinements put municipal authorities in an "indifferent financial position." Essentially the government significantly expanded the amount and permissible uses of joint national-local grants given to homeowners to improve their property and provide additional assistance for improvement of public facilities in areas where these grants would be concentrated.

As would be expected, these provisions were restrictive and well-defined, but they were facilitative rather than directly interventionist in providing for execution. In a 1972 circular sent to local authorities, the Conservative minister of housing and construction noted that a variety of methods ranging from total clearance through spot removal and area improvement to compulsory repair of individual houses would henceforth be required, according to local conditions, but, he noted, "What is most appropriate in relation to the condition of the stock and housing needs of their district is a matter for the judgement of the local authority."[85] The government promised to "sustain its support" for an approach that stressed improvement, and it surely encouraged the change in emphasis, but it did not intervene directly. In fact the chief of the department's Slum Policy Section asked me, in 1975, for information regarding Birmingham's procedures for implementing neighborhood conservation through consultation with neighborhood organizations and community groups.

The results of the department's approach for Birmingham's urban renewal program are quite clear. At first nothing changed. The city wrapped up its first phase of redevelopment and continued work on the second with no reduction in emphasis on total clearance and redesign. Planning even began for a third quite similar phase in the final set of areas identified in the postwar housing report. Although provisions of the new acts were applied in other areas of the city, areas that showed signs of structural and social stress but had never been considered for redevelopment, no major revisions in the Comprehensive Redevelopment Program were adopted. It is in fact probable that neighborhoods included in Urban Renewal would have been cleared in a third Comprehensive Redevelopment phase had the Labour group, which gained control of the City Council in 1972, not interrupted these plans (see Chapter 3). While ministry officials both in London and in Birmingham did attempt to influence Birmingham's urban renewal strategy during this period of changing policy, the lack of direct ministerial connections with the process of planning, adopting, and executing urban renewal projects meant that the changes would only be adopted when and where their adoption fit the needs and desires of local policymakers.

The contrast between the introduction of Urban Renewal in Birmingham and the Place Forez project in Lyon suggests that the differences in the structure of political relations between central and local governments found in France and Britain have a most important consequence for policymaking. French institutions, because they provide for direct intervention and require joint action, facilitate direct and immediate influence by both central and local authorities,[86] but by the same token they deny to any one agency full control over the fate of the project. British institutions, in contrast, give national agencies considerable long-run control over the programs that local agencies adopt but inhibit direct central intervention in the planning and execution of those programs. The result is a much greater potential for single local agencies to monopolize decisions about a project's content. The figure on page 56 presents a somewhat simplified picture of this contrast between French complexity and British simplicity. In Lyon several independent agencies directly influence the urban renewal program; in Birmingham the lines of influence are fewer and more tightly focused.

This contrast poses the question of central-local relations in a manner rather different from that with which we began. In each case an overall balance of political power between primarily national and primarily local institutions produces a situation in which, despite the central authorities' ultimate dominance and long-run ability to direct the flow of urban policy decisions, provincial resistance to external control and sensitivity to local political pressures are never entirely stifled or overwhelmed. French central agencies enjoy a variety of administrative, financial, and political means for making things happen in provincial cities, but Lyonnais authorities extracted considerable autonomy by deflecting, resisting, and subverting those interventions. British ministries supervise local authorities closely to be certain that precisely drawn laws and regulations are respected, but within those legal restrictions Birmingham's officials relied upon their own judgment and political will to determine the amount, timing, and substance of local actions.

What then are the implications of these different patterns of central-local relations for the substance of urban renewal policy in the two cities? American experience has led us to expect that central intervention would be a force for introducing broad social issues into policymaking and for "getting things done," for high levels of policy control. The surprising finding is that despite rather high levels of central intervention—compared, for example, to the United States—in both instances, substantial policy differences resulted from the different ways in which this control was applied. What is important in the contrast between Britain and France is less the variation in the aggregate level of

Lyon

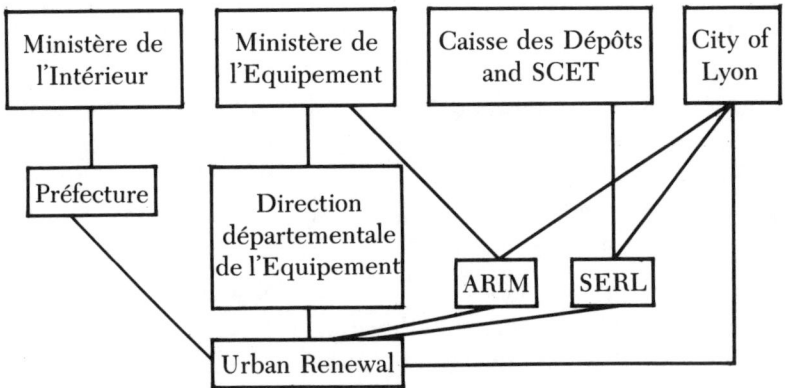

Birmingham

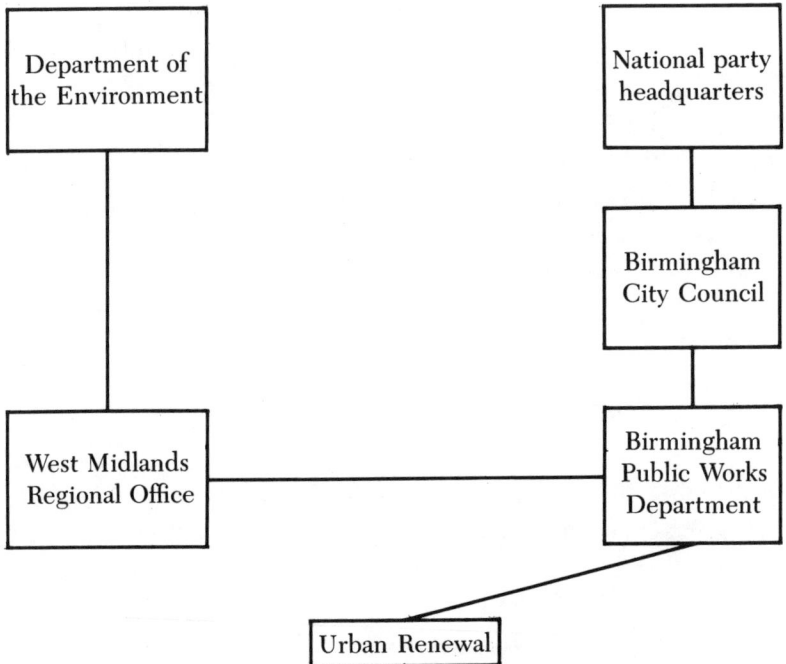

Lines of Central Intervention in Urban Renewal Projects in Lyon and Birmingham

centralization or amount of intervention in the entire system and more the variation in the number and type of political organizations at both levels that take an active part in designing and implementing urban renewal projects. Which country is more centralized does not turn out to be the most useful question for understanding policy differences. The manner of centralization has far greater implications.

National intervention was indeed a means by which major social issues were introduced into urban policymaking. In Britain programs for public provision of high-standard, low-cost housing to replace urban slums and subsequently for neighborhood conservation originated in the ministries—even Manzoni's innovations concerned strategies for expeditious implementation of existing national slum clearance programs. Similarly in France, programs for slum clearance, nieghborhood improvement, and regional economic development followed from initiatives of central government agencies concerned with urban policy issues. Thus in both cases central intervention served to introduce into local policymaking broad issues like low-income housing and economic planning that may have had no support from exclusively local political interests.

Differences in the application of central control in Britain and France do, however, help to explain striking differences in levels of policy control achieved in Lyon and Birmingham. The British pattern of local-national relations consistently stressed rule-making in London and rule applications by local authorities or, in organizational terms, it stressed a clear separation of authority between local and central agencies. Thus, while British central authorities had a lot to say about what kinds of urban renewal projects would ever be attempted, they lacked the independent political means to alter or reverse courses of action that local authorities had mapped out. In contrast, the French pattern stressed overlapping, shared, or contested control over individual projects among a mix of central and local agencies all enjoying a legal, financial, and technical base for insisting on details of design and implementation. Because the political balance among these organizations need never be resolved in any final sense for the entire course of any project but is likely to be readjusted as major issues emerge over time, several plans may be partially fulfilled and none in particular wholly accomplished.

This central contrast in national-local relations was, then, played out in Birmingham and Lyon's urban renewal projects: large projects with comprehensive, coherent plans on the one hand; small projects composed of even smaller, largely independent developments on the other. In Birmingham control over projects had been delegated to municipal officials, not shared with them as was the case in Lyon; consequently a plan would be fulfilled in Birmingham as long as local authorities remained committed to it. But projects in Lyon reflected the complex institutional and political game in which they were designed and implemented. Because different agencies at different levels of government could intervene to advance their different concerns at any point in the course of a program, projects were subject to change, compromise, and minimalist strategies. No agency had the political ability to design a plan, finance it, and impose it, and no one's plan was ever implemented.

The more general point to be stressed here concerns the role of central authorities in "getting the job done." A high level of central intervention in urban issues does not necessarily prevent the division of major projects into parcels that satisfy a variety of concerned parties but fail to form a consistent whole themselves. Not altogether surprisingly, the various agencies of central intervention quickly became interested parties themselves to the extent of their direct involvement, and their involvement may well have reduced rather than heightened the probability of fulfilling a plan. In this case, as appeared in Lyon, rather than organizing a political game that resolves policy issues and commits the state to a specific set of goals, these central agencies simply become another set of bullies disrupting the political playground.

Partisanship and Bureaucracy

3

Controlling Urban Political Fragmentation

The modern city exists so that reserves of capital, labor, and machinery may be readily combined and recombined in the ebbs and flows of industrial production. But by serving as the efficient assembly point for these productive factors, the city becomes a focus for the diversity of interests, prejudices, and aspirations harbored by the men and women who must live and work within its boundaries. This diversity is, in turn, translated into features of the physical and social face of the city itself in the shape of class or ethnically segregated neighborhoods, expressways and mass transit routes, skyscrapers and commercial centers. Where the free market operates, decisions made individually to buy, sell, invest, or consume accumulate to account for the bulk of these features, but others, as we have seen, can only result from governmental decisions to use public resources and authority for purposes that affect at once large numbers of—willing and unwilling—urban dwellers.

When crucial decisions about the city become public, the problem arises of mobilizing sufficient support for the government among sufficient numbers of the city's population so that the inevitable disruption and expense of public projects may be imposed. This process of uniting such diverse interests gives urban politics its complex and distinctive character. The present chapter seeks to identify those institutional conditions that facilitate or inhibit the development of local political support sufficient for a large-scale commitment to urban renewal.

The difficulty of achieving this unity has particularly occupied the attention of the observers of American municipal politics, and some attention to their conclusions will help set the stage for comparing the French and the British cities. In examining the politics of what must be the world's most diverse city, Wallace Sayre and Herbert Kaufman capture this central political problem: "No single group of participants in the city's political contest is self-sufficient in its power to make decisions or require decisions of others. Every decision of importance is consequently the product of mutual accommodation. Building temporary or lasting alliances, working out immediate or enduring settlements between allies or competitors, and bargaining for an improved position in the decision centers are the continuing preoccupations of all leaders—whether party leader, public leaders, public officials, leaders of organized bureaucracies, or leaders of nongovernmental groups."[1] Because, Sayre and Kaufman argue, large numbers of people inside and outside of New York City care deeply for reasons of ethnicity, wealth, partisanship, personal ambition, and neighborhood loyalty what actions leaders of that city take, any action at all becomes difficult. Any action will bear a heavy burden of accommodation and thus promote nothing else quite as much as it promotes the status quo.

Diversity inheres in the industrial city and must affect its governance, but scholars have argued that the political structure of American cities severely exacerbates this tendency toward indecision and inaction in ways perhaps not found in French or British cities. After considering a series of major issues in Chicago, Edward Banfield sums up the political context of decision making by saying, "The Chicago area from a *purely formal standpoint*, can hardly be said to have a government at all. There are hundreds, perhaps thousands, of bodies, each of which has a measure of legal authority and none of which has enough of it to carry out a course of action which other bodies oppose." As a result of this dispersion of authority, "from a formal standpoint, virtually nothing can be done if anyone opposes—and, of course, everything is always opposed by someone—and therefore every opponent's terms must always be met if there is to be action. Every outcome must therefore be an elaborate compromise if not a stalemate."[2] Thus American cities are not only politically divisive because they are socially diverse, but also because their governance is usually divided among the municipality, at least one county, a state, the federal government, and a variety of independent or quasi-independent boards, commissions, and special districts. Any really important project is likely to fall under the jurisdiction of several.

Douglas Yates has summed up these arguments: "Given its present political organization and decision-making process, the city is fundamentally ungovernable. By ungovernable I mean that it is incapable of producing coherent decisions, developing effective policies, or implementing state or federal programs."[3] The city is the last political arena, in other words, in which the synoptic ideal is likely to be realized.

Of course public projects are undertaken in New York and Chicago and other cities despite all these social and legal divisions. Cities are able to adopt and implement public policies if and when their political systems muster the support or acquiescence of participants who are capable of blocking the projected action. In practice this mobilization of support often involves the attachment of these diverse groups and organizations to a smaller group of leaders who have found within the political system ways of attracting and retaining a reasonably enduring loyalty.

Robert Dahl, for example, writing of urban renewal in New Haven, argues that "rapid, comprehensive change in the physical pattern of a city is a minor revolution" and that "the pattern of independent sovereignties with spheres of influence," which had dominated New Haven's politics, "was incapable of providing centralized, deliberated coordination over a wide range of city activities—and hence was unsuited to the task of carrying through urban redevelopment and renewal on a massive scale." Not until a new mayor achieved an "executive-centered coalition" as the strongest force in redevelopment decision making was significant action possible.[4]

To put the same matter the other way around, Alan Altshuler concluded from a study of Minneapolis and Saint Paul that in the absence of a local "power elite," the political processes of urban planning lead to "fragmenting policy choices rather than integrating them" and to "a 'project' rather than a 'general planning' orientation and a disinclination to deal with controversial issues."[5] The occasional Richard Lee or Robert Moses[6] is, then, one possible, albeit temporary, solution to the problem of dispersed power and authority.

Banfield suggests another solution, which is particularly important for comparative purposes because it involves an organization, presumably more durable and predictable than an individual. A course of public policy can only be pursued, argues Banfield, by any political actor, "insofar as the formal decentralization is somehow overcome by informal centralization. By far the most important mechanism by which this is done is the political party or machine."[7] Although Banfield does not extend this conclusion himself, the clear implication must be that cities with strong, durable political parties controlling access to city offices will be governed by a more centralized process of decision making than cities where such an organization is lacking. Furthermore, the former category of cities should exhibit more of a tendency, in Altshuler's words, to integrate rather than fragment policy problems, to plan in a more general rather than limited manner, and to approach synoptic policymaking.

If a small number of political parties can unite broad sections of the city's population behind an enduring set of principles or an enduring distribution pattern for the perquisites of office,[8] then the party qua organization can compete for citizens' loyalty with residential, ethnic, or economic ties and can offer the political basis for public action. Where local parties dominate officeholding, higher levels of policy control will be achieved in public programs.

This last point leads to another likely result of partisan control of urban politics: its effect upon the content of local programs. In reality party affiliations do not compete with loyalties to class, ethnic group, or principle; they parallel them. Parties attract durable support by packaging sets of particular appeals.

Comparative studies of large numbers of cities usually show that it is difficult to predict specific positions on policy issues from the relative strength of local parties.[9] Nevertheless, familiarity with the organizational and ideological bases of parties in different cities often provides quite a revealing perspective from which to explain different approaches to a similar undertaking.[10] Furthermore, the failure of partisan strength to account for different approaches to public projects in a cross-section of many cities in no way suggests that major shifts in relative strength among the parties in any one city will not bring about shifts in policies adopted in that city.

Comparisons of the organizational and ideological positions of political parties in Lyon and Birmingham ought therefore to lead to inferences about the impact of partisan differences on the substantive differences in major public projects like urban renewal. Do, for example, the fairly clear left-right differences in French and British parties affect the location and eventual use of urban renewal projects as different parties gain and lose influence in local politics?

Many of the previously mentioned conclusions about the effects of local politics on urban policy formulation and implementation are based on speculation and inference from particular cases. To evaluate these general propositions more fully, the next task is to look closely at the way Lyon and Birmingham are governed and then back at their urban renewal efforts.

Political structure is not immutable. Different aspects are more or less difficult to change. But when change does occur and the positions of the political organizations that support the political structure are significantly altered, conflict results, sparks fly, and observers hear strong language. Birmingham offers the opportunity to see such a change in the pattern of political conflict and also to see the effects of that change on a major area of public policy. Consequently, I treat Birmingham before 1972 and Birmingham after 1972 almost like two separate political systems before turning to Lyon.

Birmingham before 1972

Much as compartmentalization of British local and national authorities characterized the division of responsibilities for promoting urban revival, Birmingham's own political system exhibited, before a significant restructuring in 1972, an equally well articulated division of responsibilities among its political institutions. And much as British local-central relations were structured around delegation of well-defined tasks to the local authorities with little interference by central agencies, Birmingham long accepted the practice of delegation of local policy formulation and execution to technically and politically independent professional agencies. The results of compartmentalization also were similar: a stable coalition of local professional departments dominated the formulation and implementation of urban renewal plans, and few nonprofessional interests or viewpoints were allowed to affect any but the very earliest planning stages of the programs. Plans once adopted were implemented as designed.

Party Discipline and the City Council

The first of several components of Birmingham's political system that made possible this degree of control in urban renewal policy was, as the American experience predicted, the strength of local political parties. The two or three largest political parties provided the focus, the force for aggregating and directing local political interests, that was found lacking in American urban politics. This focusing power derived first from the well-known pervasive strength of British national political parties, and second, from the concomitant strength of these parties at the local level.

In the mid-1960s, while Birmingham actively pursued its Comprehensive Redevelopment plans, some 90 percent of British adults identified themselves with one of the three national political parties, and 90 percent of these people considered themselves either Labour or Conservative.[11] In contrast to the quarter of American electors who call themselves independent, no large group of Britons eligible to vote considered themselves independent of national party divisions.[12] More important for present concerns, over 90 percent of those who professed a partisan identification voted in accordance with that identification in elections for municipal offices.[13] This exceedingly high level of partisanship in the electorate provided a firm foundation from which local politicians could build a sizable, stable coalition to support efforts to command municipal offices.

The goal of local parties in municipal elections in the largest cities resembled that of their national counterparts: control of a city council composed of men and women elected (councillors) or, before the 1974 reorganization of local government, also appointed by the council (aldermen) to represent a large number of local constituencies called wards. In annual elections (except, after 1974, every fourth year when metropolitan county council elections are held) voters selected among candidates for one of three council seats for their ward and granted successful candidates a three-year term of office; aldermen were selected for six-year terms. Voters had no other choices to make; the honorific post of mayor, the leadership of council party groups, the council committee chairmanships, and the chief executive positions in the city's administration were all awarded by vote of the council. The limited scope of the voters' franchise and the rigorous partisanship of electors produced a local policymaking process in which the political parties played a pivotal role.

This electoral cleavage would, however, be insufficient to focus the diversity of interests that surround urban policy issues if local politicians did not also develop ways to organize themselves and political conflict around these partisan poles. In Birmingham, like most other large British cities, the support of one of the three major parties was virtually the only route to a seat on the city council, and party activists were certain to limit this support to candidates who had been carefully screened for party commitment and loyalty to leadership.[14]

The effectiveness of this limitation is clear from the failure of independent candidates to win election even within the quite small universe of one urban ward: at no time in the past four decades have more than three nonpartisan or local party politicians (out of 156 members before the 1974 reorganization and 126 after) sat simultaneously on Birmingham's city council; all others have been either Conservative, Liberal, or Labour party representatives.

Councillors were no more independent of party ties once they reached council chambers. Birmingham's council, like virtually all other urban councils, conducted its business like a little Parliament, according to the rewards and penalties of party discipline.[15] Prior to each council meeting, members met with the other councillors of their party, the Party Group,[16] perhaps with nonmember party officials or trade union representatives as observers, to consider the council's agenda and to determine, by vote when necessary, the group's collective positions on issues to be decided.

Councillors were bound to vote in the council meetings as these caucuses dictated. When the result of a council vote could not be affected, some councillors were permitted for reasons of conscience or to avoid supporting a measure seemingly detrimental to their own wards to abstain from voting. But as one Tory leader explained to me, "If your conscience pricks you too often, you may be in the wrong party." Because of the wide acceptance of party discipline, Birmingham political leaders could list several instances of councillors excluded or nearly excluded from their party group (permanent exclusion would ultimately deny a councillor renomination by his ward party) because they refused to support a group position, but no one could name a councillor who was denied renomination by his ward party organization because he had, by bowing to the party whip, voted against the interests of the ward.

The practical result of party discipline in the city council was that the councillors in each group subjugated their varied economic, neighborhood, and ideological differences to an overriding attachment to the party. Various factions and coalitions of factions may at different times win the group's support, but once defeated, councillors found resignation the only alternative to (at least temporary) acquiescence.[17]

Disciplined party groups provide an institutionalized process for aggregating or suppressing diverse points of view on public policy issues; they do not account for the planning and execution of specific courses of action.

Delegation and Specialization

Like any other large representative assembly, the Birmingham City Council provided an adequate forum for debate of policy issues and for ratification of projects presented to it; it could not, however, have been expected to perform the detailed work of legislation. Recognizing this limitation, the Birmingham council had adopted by 1850 a set of procedures more like those of the United States Congress than the British Parliament.

The council could, and for the most part did, adopt the broad outlines of a program and then delegate the specific decisions about content and implementation to specialized committees of its members.[18] Furthermore, the council established a set of professional departments parallel to the committees and staffed them with the technical personnel needed for both the planning and the implementation of programs within the various specialities: public works, housing management, and education. This pattern of delegation to specialists—both professional and elected—is the second major component of Birmingham's local political structure and is among the most important factors shaping the course of urban renewal in Birmingham.

Delegation of policy formulation and execution was possible within the context of partisan polarization because the parties' balance in the council and their rules of discipline were transposed to the committee operations as well. The chair and a majority of committee seats always belonged to the majority party;[19] major committee votes always divided along party lines. Consequently, the party positions could be translated both into major policy commitments and into the more routine decisions encountered in the course of implementing those policies. As James Sharpe has remarked in this context, "The differences between parties, especially British parties, may be measured not only by their clear-cut stands on specific issues but also by implicit, generalized attitudes about equality, prudent public spending, helping the underdog and the virtues of private enterprise."[20] In short, the committees provide the party groups with influence over the guts of policy issues without placing inordinate demands on the time and abilities of the council at large.[21]

There is a major discrepancy, however, between this picture of strict partisanship reaching down to decisions about sewers and paving stones and the persistence of Birmingham's Comprehensive Redevelopment Program through several changes in the party controlling the city council[22] and the council committee, Public Works, that oversaw the work. Any one of these changes could have resulted (as the 1972 change finally did) in a total overhaul of ongoing plans. And yet, despite the importance of the Comprehensive Redevelopment Program (it was one of Birmingham's largest and most costly postwar undertakings), the local Conservative Party and the faction in control of the Labour Party through 1970 simply agreed that the projects should be pursued as originally adopted. Although it was apparent that Comprehensive Redevelopment violated accepted Tory principles by substituting public for private ownership of much of Birmingham's low-cost housing and that it would damage the Labour Party's electoral position by moving thousands of Labour votes to suburban communities, neither party attempted to alter either the basic approach or the accepted procedures of Comprehensive Redevelopment.

Comprehensive Redevelopment escaped partisan attack for

two reasons. First, local issues that divided the two major parties were limited and explicit; they excluded Comprehensive Redevelopment. Tories and Labourites at both the national and the local levels squared off on matters including the sale of municipal housing units and other municipally held property, the employment of the city's own construction workers, and the organization of secondary education.[23] Although the stakes for these matters may seem rather small—between 1966 and 1972 the Tories were able to sell fewer than 1,000 of Birmingham's some 125,000 municipal housing units—they occupied the attention of group and committee leaders, who were able to agree about substantively more significant matters. These explicitly partisan issues also held the attention and concern of national party officials. The second reason for bipartisan support of Comprehensive Redevelopment underlies the first: the technical and political strength and acumen of the local administrative corps, and in particular of the Public Works Department.

The Public Works Department

It is not unusual for an administrative agency, which must be familiar with the technical possibilities of a venture, to set the agenda for adoption of public policy efforts, and it is not unusual for such agencies to implement a program in a way that leaves the agency's mark on the results. What is remarkable about Birmingham's Comprehensive Redevelopment Program was the ability of officials in the Public Works Department to design a set of projects and then see them through to completion without significant interruption.

The key to understanding this unusual tendency toward synoptic policymaking lies in the combination of partisanship and technical expertise. In his study of metropolitan Stockholm, Thomas Anton argues that "the national electoral linkage has limited the ability of local interests to enforce their preferences on local office-holders."[24] The result, he continues, is what I call policy compartmentalization: "Freedom from electoral constraints was matched by insulation of political and administrative leaders from most partisan controversy, which reduced the power of partisanship in the shaping of policy. Ritualization of partisanship, coupled with the structurally guaranteed participation of independent professional administrators, created a policy environment in which professional values and techniques dominated the role conceptions of all members of the government elite. This was and remains crucial, not only because of its impact on the substance of urban policy, but more importantly because, among a small and permanently interacting elite, professional ideologies helped to create a powerful *achievement motivation.*" [25]

Similarly, the most significant result of delegation was the compartmentalization of urban renewal policymaking within the Public Works Department, and in fact the most important result of party discipline came to be its role in protecting this agency from the many groups and individuals interested in the redevelopment of Birmingham's central areas. (The role of nongovernmental organizations is explored in detail in Chapter 4.) Accordingly, an understanding of the Public Works Department and its position within Birmingham's political structure is the key to understanding two and a half decades of Comprehensive Redevelopment.

The strength and independence of the Public Works Department rested on two crucial features of its relationship with other political organizations: internal control of staffing and widespread acceptance of the department's technical capacity and political neutrality. Vote of the city council filled only two positions in the department, that of chief officer and his deputy; bureau chiefs and administrative and technical officials were appointed by the chief officer. Moreover, like civil servants in British central ministries, chief municipal officers did not serve at anyone's pleasure; their positions were permanent, unassailable except by formal disciplinary action.

Thus despite several changes in control of the city council, Birmingham had only two chief Public Works Department officers bewteen 1935 and 1974. Herbert Manzoni was promoted from deputy to chief officer in 1935 by a Conservative-controlled city council; Manzoni chose Neville Borg, a bureau chief, as his deputy. When Manzoni retired in 1963, a Labour-controlled council elevated Borg to chief officer. Borg then held the position through two changes in party control until the Public Works Department was abolished in the 1974 nationwide reorganization of local government.

The pervasive assumption that professional officers were the neutral servants of their elected masters made possible and even reinforced the effects of this tenure system. As Sayre and Kaufman point out, the most important "strategic method" for a bureaucracy wishing to secure its autonomy is "to secure wide acceptance of an inviolate status, a taboo against 'political interference' or the intervention of 'special interests.' Once armed with this status, the organized bureaucracy can assert boldly . . . a claim to freedom from supervision."[26]

I asked a former Conservative leader if he had not been suspicious of Labour-appointed professionals when he gained control of the council. "They quite accept 'The king is dead; long live the king' idea," he replied and continued by describing his loss of access to officers upon losing his majority six years later. A retired chief officer put the same matter the other way around by claiming that both parties "have had a tacit understanding that what was good for 'Brummagen's' material welfare had to be arranged," meaning that the professional officers' "objective, technical" view of the city's welfare had never seriously been questioned. No politician, even those who came to reject the Public Works Department's approach to urban renewal, failed to praise the technical competence of the department's officers, and until 1972 no council or committee questioned the department's responsibility for the long-run, broad outlines of urban renewal policy.

Of course, central ministries, like municipal departments, are staffed with permanent, reputedly objective civil servants, and yet changes in control of Parliament regularly produce major changes in policy direction, regardless of departmental positions.[27] Several differences between ministers and chairmen and between civil servants and municipal officers account for this contrast. First of all, municipal officers, like the one just cited, accept the role of policy advocate more readily and more successfully than do civil servants.[28] In addition, part-time councillors simply have no access to the independent policy research channels that the national party organizations provide their parliamentary leadership. The technical opinion of the municipal officers was "inviolable" in part because it was the only one available. Thus when an established partisan issue was at stake—the sale of municipal houses for example—the officer's own opinions were irrelevant and bureaucratic neutrality the order of the day.

A former Birmingham town clerk[29] described the results of this professional autonomy for the process of policymaking in Birmingham. A project begins as the chief officer's idea; he convinces the committee chairman who convinces the group leader who makes sure of committee and finally council approval. Because of delegation, the remaining tasks of realizing the project are in the hands of the committee chairman and the chief officer.

Again, it is not remarkable that men and women hired for their technical training and expertise could dominate the planning and execution of a complex and technically challenging matter like urban renewal or even that they should be the usual source for innovation and the generation of major policy alternatives. What is remarkable in the case of the Birmingham Public Works Department, its relationship with other political organizations, and its role in the Comprehensive Redevelopment Program was the extent to which department officials also monopolized the choice of major directions in which the city would commit its resources and authority.

The council's adoption in 1945 and 1957 of Manzoni's plans for Central Area Redevelopment provided only for perimeters of action and not for the details of preservation, resiting, and rebuilding. Formally the committee system provided elected officials ample opportunity to criticize and amend plans for each neighborhood and thereby affect the level of control and the substance of redevelopment.

The ongoing relationship between the Public Works Department and the Public Works Committee prevented such changes from occurring. As one Conservative leader, himself critical of Birmingham's "municipalization" of the housing market, remarked, "We were caught up in the rolling of the machine." One of his colleagues, equally critical, lamented that Tory chairmen "took on the cloak of their office" and supported ongoing projects. While a former Public Works Department chief officer conceded that council leaders had "almost dictatorial powers" for deciding highly specific cases,[30] he maintained that "matters are so technical that 99 percent of the time they [committee members] cannot argue against the weight of our technical arguments. There is too much detail for them to handle. This is especially true of the big schemes. We'll present a scheme, and they'll demonstrate they're awake by objecting to the demolition of some corner pub—which we're happy to concede—or they'll only make very general comments." New leaders and chairmen are always frustrated, he said, by their inability to change things.

As we shall see presently, councillors could, in fact, have changed things. Instead they chose to protect the unity of both parties and the redevelopment plans by maintaining support for the department's projects and corralling the various economic and neighborhood interests that might have preferred different approaches to urban renewal. Accordingly, committee members concerned themselves with the details and casework—like the corner pub—that sprang from the dislocations of urban renewal and provided a channel for informing and convincing the council at large.

This allocation of technical and political tasks is what I mean by the "compartmentalization" of urban renewal policymaking in Birmingham. Without interference from council chambers or from London, one agency was permitted to plan, develop, and implement programs for the comprehensive redevelopment of Birmingham's deteriorating neighborhoods.

In the context of this political structure for policymaking, it is no longer surprising that the Comprehensive Redevelopment Program rated so high in measures of control. Birmingham's political structure allowed policymakers to consider broad, inclusive categories of subject matter (i.e., houses and commercial structures built within certain designated periods) uniformly and to treat those subjects uniformly, with only minor instances of derogation and special pleading. Entrusting planning and execution to one highly autonomous organization certainly disposes a program toward a high level of policy control.

Compartmentalization had a similar implication for the content of Comprehensive Redevelopment. Once sectional interests were reasonably well controlled, the Public Works Department could proceed along the most logical (begin with the oldest buildings) and most administratively convenient (use the national housing statutes to redevelop cleared land) lines of action. These considerations, along with rigid national construction requirements and subsidy guidelines, rather than successive victories of the Conservative and Labour parties, determined the substance, the location, and subsequent use of the Comprehensive Redevelopment projects. As we have seen, the compartmentalization of the political structure protected the program from the objections of the right; only when the political structure changed did the objections of the left come to reorient the entire renewal affair.

Birmingham after 1972

No law prevented councillors from taking an active critical role in the planning and management of Comprehensive Redevelopment; no law demanded that councillors eschew appeals to the particular problems of particular neighborhoods and tie their political fate to the city-wide and even nationwide fortunes of their parties. Councillors marched in close order because a few political organizations had the power to structure local politics around their doing so. But with swings in party popularity and the aging of long-time officeholders, the balance of political power shifted in Birmingham, the strength of organizations changed, the political structure for creating public policy changed, and the substance of urban renewal policy changed as well. In the early 1970s two structural changes occurred in Birmingham's municipal politics that had particular implications for urban renewal. One involved the relationship between councillors and their wards, the other the relationship between council committees and municipal administrative departments.

The Rise of Community Politics

The proximate cause of these changes was the series of bleak electoral years that Labour councillors suffered in the late 1960s. A thirty-seven-seat Labour advantage gained in the city council elections of 1964 had dwindled to a four-seat deficit by 1966 and had been replaced with a ninety-seat Conservative majority by 1969.[31] A particularly galling aspect of these defeats had been the reemergence of the Liberal Party, which had held no council seats since World War II, as a significant rival in municipal elections. Although Liberals never held more than eight seats, their victories occurred in the previously dependable Labour wards and relied, so politicians of all parties agreed, on unorthodox methods of cultivating neighborhood constituencies.[32]

This last point came to be very important. The leader of the local Liberal Party claimed he had been successful in local elections "because I had concerned myself with people's personal problems. . . . We Liberal Councillors have to try to be sociologists."[33] Leaders of the Conservative and Labour parties accepted this claim and spoke of it with whitened knuckles. The Liberals, said one Labour chairman, depended upon "supposed community politics and ward work with no policies whatsoever." They would move into Labour areas "like nomads" and defeat Labour councillors. A Conservative leader spoke with equal shock: "Liberals always tried to do a policy of what I'd call 'grassroots.' They were always after little problems. At public meetings the Liberals wanted to discuss someone's blocked drain. Or they'd see on the committee agenda that some street was due several months hence for resurfacing, and they'd go there asking people to sign a petition if they wanted their street resurfaced. Then when the decision was published, they'd go back and say 'See what I did for you.'" Even allowing for a large dose of partisan rivalry, we can see in these comments the scorn of men who feel that accepted practices have been violated and violated successfully.

The Liberals themselves never gained an electoral base sufficient to challenge the two-party domination of the city council. But because their successes occurred exclusively in supposedly safe Labour wards, which were also the areas most heavily affected by Comprehensive Redevelopment, Liberal victories did have an effect upon strategies adopted by other parties, especially Labour, and thereby had an effect on urban renewal policy.

The Labour leader just cited admitted that the Liberal successes "prompted" Labour Party councillors to be more attentive to the needs of individuals in their wards and to secure organizational bases at the neighborhood level. From perhaps a more objective viewpoint, a senior Public Works officer commented that "the success of Liberals based on local ward-level issues and problems" had ensured "the sensitivity of the politician to his local area. He knows that if he doesn't get improvements he'll be discredited." The contrast to a one-time Conservative councillor who told me, "No one's going to vote for you because their road got fixed," is remarkable. Once the pattern of conflict for electoral office had changed from general attachment to party to include concern over the particular problems of specific neighborhoods, changes in the process of making public policy followed quickly.

The source of these changes was the new generation of Labour members who were elected to the city council. The combination of electoral devastation in the late 1960s with the rise of neighborhood-oriented election strategies had allowed a substantial number of novices to win Labour nominations for the council and then to profit from Labour electoral successes in 1970, 1971, 1972, and 1973 (for the reorganized council that took office in March 1974). In 1972, when Labour took control of the council with 96 of the 154 seats, only 32 of its number had held a council seat before 1970, the year the Labour comeback began. The same group would dominate the Birmingham Metropolitan District Council from its creation in 1974 until 1976.

The new councillors had, by their own report, won nomination and election by developing popular and organizational support within a selected set of wards that had traditionally elected Labour councillors, that had defected to the Liberals or Conservatives, and that had undergone or were projected to undergo Comprehensive Redevelopment. The Liberals had already discovered and were presumed to have based their electoral success on the widespread discontent engendered by the disruptions, dislocations, and readjustments that accompanied redevelopment.[34] The neighborhood work of aspiring Labour politicians unearthed the same sentiments and added a specific concern with urban renewal to their community politics approach. The result was that in 1972 control of the city council passed to a group of councillors who were less fully attached to accepted council practices, more attached to ward-level organizations, and more concerned with urban renewal than were their predecessors.

The Decline of Compartmentalization

One additional reagent must be added to this formula for political change: technical expertise within the council group. I argued that the strength and autonomy of the Public Works Department depended in large measure upon its reputation among local politicians for high technical competence and public-interested neutrality. The new council members elected in the

early 1970s were not only more aware of the political implications of urban renewal, they were more aware of its technical
possibilities as well. As one senior engineer described them,
"The politicians are better informed than twenty years ago.
Manzoni couldn't have gotten away with many things if they had
been." Of particular importance was the election in 1970 of a
quantity surveyor, Brian Shuttleworth, as a Labour councillor
from an inner city ward.[35]

Using his own experience in building and construction planning and his contacts with outside sources of expertise, Shuttleworth began, with a study group drawn from the Labour
Group, to evaluate redevelopment and alternative approaches
to decayed urban neighborhoods. Not surprisingly for politicians, members of this study group, the Urban Renewal Conference, came to regard deteriorating neighborhoods as collections of citizens and voters rather than, as the engineers of the
Public Works Department tended to see them, collections of
structures that served a changing group of people.

The significance of this development lies in its effect on the
relationship between the council and the department. Once the
department lost its monopoly on expertise and once alternative
views of urban renewal entered the public agenda, the department was no longer neutral—it had its own party line to which
others might be opposed—and its technical word could be questioned as well. Once the department was no longer inviolable,
outsiders could "interfere" with its work. And interfere they did;
the result was the Urban Renewal Program.

Let us assemble the pieces of these changes in political structure and urban renewal policy. At a time when voices from a
variety of directions were speaking of the value of the urban
community, however poor its physical facilities might be, and
advocating the participation of such communities in planning
their own futures,[36] the Birmingham Labour Party found itself
under immediate electoral pressure to move in a neighborhood-
oriented organizational direction. In doing so, politicians found

Comprehensive Redevelopment to be a policy that was bound to disrupt grassroots political organizations and further alienate voters.[37] These considerations provided the motivation, and the development of alternative sources of expertise provided the means, for an attack on the Comprehensive Redevelopment Program and the process through which it was adopted and implemented.

Accordingly, Shuttleworth and the Urban Renewal Conference seized upon neglected provisions of the 1969 housing act to prepare an alternative renewal plan based on (1) retention and improvement of existing structures and (2) the direct participation of block and neighborhood organizations in planning the renewal of specific areas of the city. When the Labour Group took control of the council in 1972, the second phase of redevelopment was (marginally) reduced and plans for a third phase were scrapped. Despite their resistance to both the proposals and the methods of implementing them, senior officers were required to appear before vociferous neighborhood meetings and develop renewal plans in joint professional-politician-citizen committees. The change in political structure that lay behind these policy developments was formalized in the local government reorganization of 1974 when the Public Works Department was divided into several smaller departments and its chief and deputy chief officers allowed to take early retirement.

The change in political structure that occurred between 1970 and 1974 partially broke up Birmingham's compartmentalized policymaking process and substituted a pattern of dispersed authority and expertise over certain specific aspects of urban renewal policy. The result was a new program that reflected in its substance the political change that had occurred. Control, by design, was lower than for Comprehensive Redevelopment. Plan fulfillment and project size had to be reduced when decisions about demolition and retention were being made by residents' vote, block by block. Similarly, physical change was reduced once local residents were offered subsidies, as the 1969 housing act provides, for the improvement of their homes. And finally, selection of sites for action, in such a decision-making context, of course, reflected the interests of neighborhood residents, regardless of larger questions of the development of the city as a whole. Urban Renewal represented a major reorientation of public policy; a change in political structure lay behind that reorientation.

Policymaking is always a political process because choices must involve judgments, however implicit, about justice, social progress, the balance among competing social groups, and the way public decisions ought to be made. Before 1972 politics in Birmingham reflected a striking separation, which I have called compartmentalization, of these judgments. In particular citizens' preferences were hardly ever allowed to impinge upon professional, technical opinions about the way urban renewal would be carried out. Note how local political organizations reflected this separation: political parties dealt with shifting mass preferences by offering distinct, if somewhat abstract, choices to voters but avoiding most substantive questions of local policy; professional departments remained ostentatiously nonpartisan but developed, selected, and implemented the basic features of local projects.

As the changes that took place after 1972 showed, this extent of compartmentalization was possible because party leaders did not believe that choices about the substance of policy issues would significantly affect their chances for electoral success. The resources and expertise needed to plan and implement urban renewal could, therefore, be entrusted to a single, unified department like Public Works. Once, however, politicians began to suspect that local issues could be decided in ways that would produce votes, the partisan, electoral compartment began to leak into its professional-policy neighbor. Councillors now insisted that electors' preferences, as well as professional opinions, be considered in making policy choices and that planning and implementation be distinguished, considered separately, and assigned to different groups of administrators.

Lyon

If the process that began in Birmingham in the early 1970s had continued and the overlap of organizations making political judgments had spread, policymaking in Birmingham might have come to resemble what we see in Lyon. In fact, the Labour Party managed to incorporate "community politics" into its candidate selection process and thereby managed to squeeze out further attempts to build local political support independent of the national political parties. Using the Urban Renewal Program as a compromise, the local Labour Party allowed only a limited and specific change in the local political structure. Because national party attachments rather than appeals to Birmingham's indigenous cleavages remained the basis for electoral success, popular support and policymaking remained largely separate.[38]

For Lyon, on the other hand, this firm allegiance to national political parties was not available as a solution to the potential divisiveness of urban politics, nor did a unified professional approach ever dominate the planning and execution of urban renewal as one had in Birmingham. As a result, shifting alliances and multiple points of access characterized policymaking in Lyon, much as such a process had characterized the relationship between local and national political organizations. These contrasts mark the second step toward understanding the differences in the substance of urban renewal in the two cities.

The first contrast in political structure between the two cities brings us back to the fundamental urban political problem of building a durable basis of political support out of a city's jumble of competing groups and interests. For policymakers in Birmingham the problem was for the most part solved because allegiances to the national political parties produced ready-made coalitions—at both mass and elite levels—that supported and gave considerable freedom to local leaders. By necessity and by design, however, politicians in Lyon turned to a rather different kind of solution.

In part a different solution was the inevitable result of the great differences between French and British political parties and in particular of differences at the grass roots. In the first place, while some 90 percent of British electors identified themselves with a national political party, less than 45 percent responded similarly in France.[39] That fact alone means that even if those party preferences were automatically translated into votes for party slates in municipal elections, as occurs in Britain, more than half of all potential voters would still be undecided. But voting patterns suggest that this translation is made in a highly imperfect way.[40] In the early years of the Fifth Republic, for example, candidates with the Gaullist label who had considerable success in contesting seats in the Chamber of Deputies were systematically unsuccessful in gaining control of city hall within their constituency.[41] In later years, as voters have collected around left and right poles in national elections, they have continued to support centrist coalitions in municipal elections.[42] These findings point to a general tendency to divorce local and national political preferences.

This divorce is important for urban policymaking because it provides local politicians with political entrepreneurship opportunities that are unavailable in a British-style system. Where party support is weak, party discipline must also be weak. A skilled local politician can make and dissolve local coalitions[43] or create a personal image quite distinct from any partisan affiliations he might have.[44] Thus, except for those on the Communist list, municipal candidates tend to represent both a spectrum of local factions and interests and the ability of certain prominent politicians to unite these groups behind their leadership.[45] A successful political keystone can assure himself a pleasing longevity: from 1947 through the municipal elections of 1965, hardly a period of political doldrums, only ten of the thirty-one French cities with populations greater than 100,000 had had more than two mayors.[46]

A second source of entrepreneurship opportunities follows from the French city's complex of external relationships. The complicity we have seen between local and national officials works not only to ease the task of the central government's regulators, but also to enhance the position of the local government accomplice, particularly the mayor. Two scholars, who have carefully explored this relationship, summarize it well:

> In effect . . . the [central] administration conditions the capacity
> for action of the local elected official to the point where it is, in the
> final analysis, the administration that sanctions and consecrates
> the elected official's management as much and even more than his
> electors. But a network of administrative relations, the crucial ele-
> ment of all local power, is something that one spends a long time
> establishing, that one guards jealously, and that one is reluctant to
> share. Faced with these advantages, the newcomer, whatever his
> goodwill and the value of his ideas may be, hardly has the means
> to put them into practice. Quite rationally, the voter will prefer
> the old hand at the wheel [vieux routier] of administrative politics.
> In this way the permanence of provincial notables is established.[47]

Even without attributing this degree of rationality to voters, we can imagine the difficulties involved in mounting a challenge to a mayor whom important central government officials wished to support. For a mayor to lose his office, someone else must organize and mobilize an effective electoral challenge. When the financial and administrative authority of the central government can be enlisted to placate or co-opt potential opposition, such a challenge becomes more difficult and less likely.[48]

This personalized approach to managing urban politics is reminiscent of Dahl's executive-centered coalition: the mayor succeeds in uniting otherwise disparate political groups and interests by offering them individually some access to public decision making and collectively some chance for stable local administration and profitable relations with the central administration.

As a solution to the diversity problem, this kind of coalition has specific implications for public policy issues like urban renewal. Whereas partisanship in Britain or Sweden or influence and a dependable flow of material favors in Banfield's Chicago both use some external adhesive to bind a coalition, the executive-centered coalition can only offer its ability to use public authority in ways that defend the interests of its members. They must be satisfied with the results, or the coalition dissolves.[49] As we shall see in Lyon, this solution, because it is weaker than the one found in Birmingham, results in urban renewal that is less disruptive of the physical and social status quo and less likely to fulfill plans completely than was Birmingham's.

No better example than Lyon may be found of a French mayor's ability to form personally the keystone of a local political coalition and thereby to entrench himself in city hall. Between 1905 and 1978 only two men played this role, and they played it in very different ways.

Edouard Herriot first assumed the office of mayor of Lyon in 1905; no one else held that position until Herriot's death in 1957.[50] No case need be made for this Radical-Socialist party leader, repeated prime minister, and National Assembly president's national political and administrative connections. Within Lyon's city council (then elected by proportional representation) Herriot was able to play the mediating role that often fell to his Parti radical in national politics.

In the council, as in the National Assembly, Radicals rarely held a majority of seats, and in the later years of Herriot's mayoralty they did not even achieve a plurality.[51] Rival politicians, however, considered Herriot the only conceivable choice to preside over the council, the only politician whose personal prestige made him capable of creating a working cohesion out of these rival groups. If the threat of exclusion served to discipline the vote of Birmingham's city councillors, Herriot's repeated threats of resignation served, somewhat more modestly, to maintain support for diverse council coalitions.[52]

The importance of a man of great reputation, acceptable to a variety of local factions, became clear at Herriot's death in 1957. The council factions, which had been willing to unite behind Herriot, found themselves after lengthy discussion unable to select a successor from among rival party leaders.[53] Rather than face dissolution, the Radical group nominated one of its less prominent members, Assistant Mayor for Sport Louis Pradel, and recruited Communist and Socialist (S F I O) support for what was presumed to be a temporary solution. Pradel was elected mayor with a scant majority, and the party leaders became his assistant mayors.[54] It was anticipated that more established leaders would regroup by the 1959 elections and a permanent successor to Herriot would emerge.

Contrary to these expectations, a successor had already emerged. Upon assuming office, Pradel promptly and ostentatiously renounced all partisan affiliations and began developing personal support in local commercial, professional, and centrist trade union organizations. In addition, he seized upon a fortunate coincidence.

The reconstruction of areas damaged during World War II was, by 1957, nearing completion, and government financial and technical assistance for the redevelopment of other areas, including Lyon, was becoming available. Pradel, reversing Herriot's conservatism in local development matters, agreed to support and even become a public advocate for projects like the acquisition and redevelopment of the Part-Dieu. "Projects that could be seen," said one centrist leader. The mayor's support and the ministries' plans allowed Pradel and his nonpartisan slate to capture a plurality of council seats and the mayorality in the 1959 elections. Pradel retained that position until his death seventeen years later. By 1971 two observers could write of Pradel's disregard for national party allegiances: "Pradel had such a grip on the local vote that he could win, with or without the U D R" (Union pour la Défense de la république, the Gaullist Party).[55] In fact, according to a local opposition leader, Pradel's antipartisan stance was a major part of his local appeal.

Thus Pradel, lacking any national reputation or partisan following, adopted one variant of the strategies outlined above and built his personal support from a combination of electoral alliances with a wide range of local groups[56] and from administrative alliances with central government sources of capital and expertise. In each case the mayor himself was the binding force of the alliance. We have already seen evidence (in Chapter 2) of Pradel's influence with the central government.

Perhaps the best indication of the highly personal character of the coalition supporting Lyon's administration may be found in its name. In 1959 these nonpartisan politicians called themselves "Union et défense des intérêts de la Ville de Lyon." For the 1965, 1971, and 1977 elections the coalition's name on its campaign literature and ballot was "Pour la Réalisation active des espérances lyonnaises" or "PRADEL."[57] The name but not the overwhelming electoral support survived Pradel's death in November 1976. A significant drop in the list's vote in 1977 municipal elections is further indication that it was a personal rather than an organizational alliance.[58]

Although the PRADEL list won handily in the municipal elections of 1965 and 1971, the problem of its inherent fragility, which emerged clearly in 1977, remained important for the governance of the city. An inclusive coalition like the PRADEL list provides a broad basis of support, but it raises once again the problem that virtually no action can be taken that does not offend some section of the alliance.

Pradel's first strategy for dealing with this difficulty recognized the scant value and the potential divisiveness of partisan associations. He refused to place on the list anyone of national political reputation.[59] In addition, the mayor himself and the assistant mayors assigned to various policy areas maintained careful and personal supervision of city programs to ensure that interests crucial to the coalition were not severely offended and that no room was given to potential rivals who might attempt to mount a challenge based on disaffected groups. Thus, for example, a plan to close streets in the old city center to automobiles was subjected to lengthy consultation procedures and numerous changes of direction because delay was safer than a divisive action. An additional urban renewal project adjacent to the Part-Dieu was first warmly embraced and then quashed; as the mayor said, "Zut à la ZAC [damn the redevelopment zone]."

A pattern of political conflict like the one found in Lyon will, of course, have important implications for the institutions directly involved in making and implementing public policy. An indication of the effects of Lyon's solution to the urban political problem comes from the organization and patterns of delegation found in the municipal bureaucracy.[60] In Birmingham, when electoral pressures, perceived as local in origin, threatened the position of the Labour Party, councillors moved to decrease delegation and increase their own influence over the substance of policy issues. Since pressures of this sort appeared pervasive to Lyonnais politicians, they attentively kept their spoons in the pot of all important local programs. Once again the division of responsibility and multiplication of points of access to decision making was the rule, and control over the many tasks involved in a project like urban renewal was distributed among a variety of agencies.

Before 1964, long-range planning, studies of future development trends, and development of policy alternatives were undertaken by field agents of the central ministries. Since 1964 those tasks have been the joint work of the Direction and the Atelier d'Urbanisme (Urban Planning Studio) of the city of Lyon.[61]

Although its director was one of Pradel's most trusted advisers, the Atelier itself was never staffed nor provided the opportunity to develop and direct the details of implementation for the projects it conceived. The agency could never become a resolute and indispensable advocate of long-range commitments to policy objectives. Rather, the Atelier could only propose boundaries and basic physical characteristics (size, approximate location, and density) for proposed projects: the actual operations were the job of the SERL. We have already considered the juridical and financial advantages offered by the quasi-public corporation; by separating from long-range planning the prosaic matters of real estate transactions and specific development decisions, the SERL offered the political advantage of providing an additional arena for bargaining over the details of specific projects. Finally, the responsibility for providing public facilities—city administrative buildings, streets, sewers, sidewalks—fell to still another agency, the city's public works department.[62]

In principle a political arbiter could have coordinated these activities and directed these agencies to support mutually agreed upon plans. In practice no such arbiter emerged. The deputy director of the Atelier reported extensive contact with the long-range planning sections of the Direction, but "isolation" from the "working" services of the city itself. The Atelier therefore, was, in his opinion, fairly useful in providing information to politicians and carrying out day-to-day tasks, but incapable of setting clear development objectives for Lyon. For urban renewal, a Direction engineer argued, the planning services would produce bold "paper plans," but these were always lost in the later search for the "easiest solution."

The SERL, on the other hand, was particularly well suited to this search for solutions that would ease political difficulties. It had an aura of independence, and one of its major tasks, a SERL project director told me, was to serve as a "screen" for local politicians by taking on the difficult and unpopular jobs of expropriation and rehousing, which follow from urban renewal. Similarly SERL officials could act as referees in disputes among planners, developers, residents associations, and politicians. Throughout, Pradel himself kept close watch over the details of programs, insisting upon expressways or pedestrian streets or green areas as his political judgment dictated.

Political conflict and decision making in Lyon demanded detailed and repeated negotiations over the substance of projects and the protection of a variety of local concerns. An organization like the Birmingham Public Works Department that, under unified bureaucratic authority, controlled each of the successive phases of urban renewal would have been intolerable. Politics in Lyon demanded the isolation of details and rejected long-term commitments to broad objectives. Political leaders ultimately judged even the SERL too comprehensive an organization and assigned projects to other SEMs. When the council authorized a redevelopment project, which was in fact never carried out, for the residential areas bordering the Part-Dieu, it assigned the work to a private nonprofit development corporation independent of the S C E T network.

The division of responsibility and the perceived fragility of the governing coalition had a clear impact on each of Lyon's urban renewal projects. Both the level of control—plan fulfillment and size of projects—and the number of areas actually treated were greatly reduced as a result. The most notable instance of a low level of policy control comes from the numerous revisions of plans for the Part-Dieu and Moncey Nord areas. While early plans called for publicly directed renewal of an area almost twice the size of the sites that the geriatrics center and the military installation had vacated, the boundaries progressively shrank as opposition mounted. Publicly endorsed plans[63] for the redevelopment of surrounding residential neighborhoods lay idle and eventually died because, as the director of public works said of such projects, "the mayor doesn't like political problems." Similarly, Pradel refused to use city expropriation powers to require the restoration of all buildings at Place Forez, readily accepted plans limiting demolition at Martinière-Tolozan, and rejected redevelopment efforts in the Croix-Rousse area beyond the rather limited Grande Côte project. In the last instance, the council leaders opted to eschew the public expropriation procedures for acquiring properties in favor of the more costly but quieter expedient of buying the land through an intermediary parcel by parcel on the open market.

Because the redevelopment of densely inhabited urban neighborhoods invariably provokes discord and opposition, the fragility of Lyon's political coalition provided a strong incentive simply to restrict the compass of such programs. The contrast between the patterns of political conflict in Lyon and Birmingham is reflected in the contrasting patterns for making and implementing public policy decisions. The resulting difference is another important factor in the observed contrast in plan fulfillment and a crucial explanation for the contrast in the scope of action the two cities undertook. In Birmingham it was possible for engineers and public health officials simply to trace the lines of redevelopment over large sections of the city and to do so with confidence that unified organizations would provide the tools for implementation and the political support needed to realize their projects. In Lyon the publicity surrounding the announcement of redevelopment plans provided a political dividend that could rapidly be lost in the difficulties of implementation. A progressive constriction of perimeters and withdrawal from disruptive approaches repeatedly provided the "easiest solution" for Lyon's urban renewal.[64]

Similarly, Lyon's pattern of political conflict had a major impact on the content of urban renewal policy. Redevelopment—for reasons I discuss in Chapter 5—produced substantial amounts of social and physical change in every project except Place Forez. Because this change was, in itself, a source of political strain for the governing coalition, it was impossible to consider urban renewal as a general solution for reviving the city's decaying areas. Accordingly, the major sites actually adopted were those other projects and developments made available: the subway works at Martinière-Tolozan, the closing of the geriatrics center at Moncey Nord, and the acquisition of the military installation at the Part-Dieu.

In its study of urban politics in Roanne, a group of French scholars wrote that the mayor had turned the local development plan on its head: "To a logic in which the principal term is the *economic unity* of the metropolitan area and the secondary term its political unity, he opposed a logic of centralization of *political power* in which the principal term is the *political unity* of the urban area and the secondary term is its economic unity."[65] The contrast between politics in Birmingham—at either stage—and in Lyon is a contrast between political structures in which "political unity" at the local level is or is not a problem that dominates substantive decisions about public policy.

Planning and Investment

4

Private Roles in Public Policy

The rationale for publicly sponsored renewal projects lay in the government's ability to group piecemeal private investment decisions together according to a plan. Doing so, the argument goes, allows public officials to consider the consequences of a set of investments from a broader persepective. We have already seen difficulties with considering "the government" as if it had one consistent viewpoint for evaluating alternative redevelopment strategies. The analysis now becomes more complicated as we ask to what extent various governmental actors succeeded in controlling investment in urban redevelopment projects. To what extent did the revival of the two cities become a public matter?

To say that government agencies take responsibility for matters previously in private hands is to leave a broad range for variations. Governments will carry out to different extents and in differing manners attempts to monopolize decisions about specific areas of social policy. The variation follows from the third pattern of political relationships. Like the relations between central and local governments and the patterns of competition among political contestants at these levels, relations among public and private agencies and enterprises become institutionalized during a long process of cooperation, conflict, and compromise and, becoming institutionalized, come themselves to constrain and direct the substance of public policy.

Urban renewal in Lyon and Birmingham resulted—in an immediate sense—from governmental decisions to take away from tenants, shopkeepers, landlords, homeowners, and developers the ability to decide piecemeal how the city should grow and change. Because in neither country was this the first time public authorities had decided to intervene in a previously private economic activity, the considerable weight of established organizational relations and practices set extensive ground rules for this takeover to follow. The differences in these ground rules and in the resulting takeovers form the third set of institutional contrasts that gave Lyon and Birmingham such different experiences with urban development.

The Structure of Public-Private Relations: Economic Policy in Britain and France

To lay the groundwork for a detailed consideration of relationships between public and private organizations in the context of urban renewal and to establish a framework for comparisons of the patterns these relationships may follow and have followed in Great Britain and France, some attention may usefully be paid to an area of policy in which these relationships are well developed and have also been extensively treated in scholarly analyses. A rich source for suggestions about how these relationships develop may be found in accounts of attempts to manage and direct economic growth. The idea that autonomous firms, following the lead of the market, would invest in the wrong things, at the wrong pace, and in the wrong locations has become widespread. So has the acceptance of government intervention to right those supposed wrongs. Once again, the issue arises because the costs and benefits apparent to firms making investment decisions do not match the costs and benefits most important to public authorities; governments respond by formulating an economic growth policy.

To aggregate piecemeal decisions and effect such a policy, governments have recourse to actions ranging from outright nationalization through regulation, tax incentives, and subsidies, to the provision of information about underused opportunities. The adoption and implementation of such techniques involve a continuous confrontation between public and private decision makers. Consequently the practice of economic growth policy offers us a good indication of the ongoing relations between the two sectors in any country and the extent and form of government intervention in previously private economic decisions. Thus the problems and techniques of economic policy resemble those of urban renewal. Even though policymakers may have thought they were about very different tasks (e.g., achieving good urban design in British urban renewal), they, in fact, confronted the same political problem of public-private relations.

Perhaps because the two countries have strikingly diverged in their relative abilities to stimulate and sustain economic growth, scholars have often used Great Britain and France for examples of different ways in which governments can approach an economic growth policy. Most prominent among these accounts is Andrew Shonfield's comparison of the French "conspiracy to plan" with British "arm's length government." Since World War II, general, publicly determined goals for economic growth have, Shonfield argues, been a major force directing the French economy, but have remained a negligible consideration for private firms in Britain. The reason for this contrast lies in

> the traditional British view of the proper relationship between public and private power. The two sorts of power are thought of as utterly distinct from one another. They may enter into certain formal and well-defined relationships; but they do not mingle. Here, once again, there is the profound contrast with the traditional attitude of the French. In France the mixture of public and private endeavor is accepted as being of the essence of the economic process. It was therefore characteristic and predictable that the French would use their *commissions de modernisation* as an all-purpose vehicle which would carry them in any desired direction, while the British, presented with an analogous piece of machinery, were barely able to make it move at all.[1]

Whereas French officials, "interventionist by nature and by training . . . understood it to be their business to secure a general bias in the important economic decisions, whether taken in the public or the private sector, in a given direction,"[2] their British counterparts felt "the old instinctive suspicion of positive government. . . . It was reflected both in the behavior of ministers who refused to plan and in the administrative devices invented for them by civil servants, who were anxious above all to ensure that the exercise of the new powers of government did not saddle them with the responsibility for making choices, for which they might later be accountable."[3] Economic growth had become for France a matter for public, political determination, and the firms that could produce that growth had become subject to increasing amounts of government control, support, and coercion.

No one, least of all Shonfield, would argue that British governments have kept their hands off the operation of British business; nationalized industries, extensive social services, and redistributive taxes have too pervasive an influence to be called exceptions. What Shonfield would stress, however, are the narrow, unsystematic, and uncoordinated aims of these programs. Britain has lacked support for long-term action when such a course found itself in one of its "inevitable conflicts with the short-term imperatives which are all too readily accepted by governments in moments of economic or political stress."[4] Jack Hayward, who has also contrasted French and British economic policy, argues that the British inability to establish and pursue long-range "heroic" planning goals has in fact, heightened the necessity to intervene in the economy on a short-term, piecemeal basis.[5]

While Shonfield may accurately describe a British disposition toward keeping public and private power "utterly distinct," governmental actions inevitably affect private undertakings while private sector plans must constrain the government's policy designs. French political structures explicitly build this joint action into the process of making economic policy—the French word is *concertation*. One of the principal exponents of public-private *concertation*, to whom I refer again later, François Bloch-Lainé, writes that *concertation* would reign in "a regime in which the principal options for investment, production, and exchange depend in their respective spheres on neither the heads of firms or public officials, but proceed from a permanent collaboration."[6] Significant and regularized mutual accommodation is facilitated, the distinction between public and private blurred. British structures, however, require an additional mechanism to ensure that public and private officials talk to one another about overlapping concerns. To provide this contact between the two spheres of influence, extensive and formal patterns of consultation between government agencies and representatives of private, functional interests have evolved.

The importance for the formulation of British public policy of consultation with organized groups is a familiar theme. The point is most lucidly argued by Samuel Beer, who describes an attitude found among civil servants, officials, parliamentarians, and the general public that "organized groups have a 'right' to take part in making policy related to their sector of activity; indeed, that their approval of a relevant policy or program is a substantial reason for public confidence in it and conversely that their disapproval is cause for public uneasiness. It is in short an attitude reflecting the widespread acceptance of functional representation in British political culture."[7] This, in Shonfield's words, "obsession with representation—the anti-leadership principle,"[8] requires a policymaking process in which the government indeed enters as an important participant and uses its authority accordingly. Since, however, the autonomy of private sector participants must be recognized, the government does not systematically attempt to dominate and direct the actions of other participants, much less lock the others out of the process. As a result, policy is made through a high level of consultation and negotiation, but with a low level of governmental control.[9]

Hayward, in fact, attributes the failure of successive British governments to adopt an assertive industrial policy to this requirement for representation: "Why this was not to occur can be shown by reference to the tripartite British style of government relations with business and labor, compared with French *concertation*, as well as the absence in Britain of a sufficiently strong and positive authority within the executive to overcome the forces of incrementalism and inertia, such as existed in some matters in France."[10] The contrast with French industrial policymaking is indeed striking. Hayward contrasts the "sponsor" approach of British ministries with the French role as "tutor":[11]

> Just as "sponsorship" implies the advocacy within the public decisionmaking process, by a spending department, of the demands of sectional interests in return for co-operation with public policy, while *tutelle* suggests the subordination of a ministry's clientele to the requirements of public policy in return for specific favors from a paternalistic authority, government-group relations in the two countries tend to assume different patterns. . . . [I]n matters of economic planning [French] business and labor—with certain spectacular exceptions such as incomes policy—have been powerless to prevent the sovereign government from imposing its policy preferences. Face-saving consultative procedures have been gone through to impart an air of representational legitimacy to decisions that were made well before the functional and political spokesmen of the government's "social partners" were in a position to intervene.[12]

Moreover, institutions of central government reinforce this rejection of bargaining. The French finance ministry, for example, blocks more effectively than does the British Treasury the propensity of functional departments to develop clientalistic relationships with private organizations.[13]

The point is not that French officials ignore and overpower all private interests, but that they are comparatively free, as Ezra Suleiman has written, to consider consultation "a privilege granted rather than an obligation forced on an administration."[14] Surely economic policy is realized through cooperation with private interests simply because production consists largely in the labor and capital of private sector owners, managers, and workers. That cooperation, however, will be granted or withheld in France to the extent that the private groups act to further centrally determined public policy.

One further matter is important. Whereas the British view of
functional representation tends to be extensive—groups must
be represented because they exist—the French idea of using
private organizations as instruments of policy means that contacts are much more selective. In particular, groups gain access
because they represent the "dynamic," that is, the large and
concentrated economic sectors. The logic of planning has long
led officials to favor the largest national firms and to seek further
concentration: the fewer firms, the more control; larger equals
modern equals productive.[15]

A now familiar matter is once again at issue here: differences
in political structure condition the ability of different governments to pursue similar policy matters effectively. Like relations
between and among central and local government agencies and
among local political groups, relations between and among public and private organizations affect the substance of public policy. This last relationship has particular importance in liberal societies because, on the one hand, the freedom of private citizens
and groups to act in their perceived self-interest is an almost sa-
cred political principle and, on the other hand, governments
must find ways to keep private actions consistent with public
policy lest they become merely another participant in a piecemeal decision-making process.

As we have just seen, scholars have found in Great Britain and
France two quite different solutions to this conflict and have
attributed the two countries' quite different experiences with
economic planning to these contrasting solutions. French political structure allows the government to control the private economic sector and promote public goals by intervening directly in
the decisions—especially the investment decisions—of private
firms. In contrast, British institutions promote clear distinctions
between public and private affairs, but because the ideological
and technical realities of enacting public policy must muddy the
boundaries, a complex pattern of functional representation has
come to blunt and diffuse public initiatives. France, this group

of scholars would argue, has acknowledged that public and private purposes must overlap and that public power must either confront or cooperate with private power if an economic policy is to be implemented. By rejecting this approach, Britain has rejected a potent means to achieve its policy goals.

To the extent these patterns of relationships between public officials and private organizations hold for those institutions particularly concerned with urban renewal,[16] several differences would be expected between British and French efforts. First, a much higher level of control is to be expected in France. Government officials—whether primarily national or local in affiliation—would develop plans for renewal and then enlist private firms, whose cooperation is crucial but whose submissiveness is assured, to see the plan realized. British planners would seem more likely to propose broad schemes, perhaps with major subsidies and strict regulations. Decisions about what if anything would be done, however, would be left either to action by the private sector or to carefully negotiated agreements with a wide range of private actors. Moreover, if it is correct that the French finance ministry carefully watches all major public investment efforts, we might further expect that the alliance actually made for major projects will favor the further development of dynamic, national portions of the private sector at the expense of smaller, local concerns.[17] In contrast these smaller local interests should much more effectively influence the substance of urban renewal policy in Birmingham.

I have spoken of structured relations between the public and private sectors in Britain and France as if these patterns resulted from some conscious choice; of course they do not. The relative autonomy of public and private institutions is a political matter that follows from the ability of these institutions to insist upon a given role in making public policy. In order to see if these relationships and their consequences indeed hold for urban renewal in Birmingham and Lyon, it is useful to specify conditions under which public and private policymakers are relatively more and less autonomous. With these conditions in mind, we can look once again at urban renewal in the two cities and ask how patterns of public and private relations affected the substance of these programs.

In his study of interest groups in Italian politics, Joseph LaPalombara distinguishes between two kinds of relationships between private groups and governmental organizations and considers conditions that result in the former gaining influence over public policy. The first relationship, which LaPalombara calls *clientela*, requires the public agency concerned to have "a *technical* need for information; a *political* need to domesticate to some extent the object of administrative regulation; *a value orientation* implying that the administrative agency exists in part to help or assist the objects regulated; some *structural deficiencies* in the administrative agency that make it impossible or unlikely that it can secure information on its own initiative and from its own resources; and finally, the *sociopsychological* need of maintaining an orderly and reasonable predictive relationship between the agency and the groups affected by its actions."[18] The second relationship, *parentela*, involves groups that are attached to a dominant political party and that can use that attachment as leverage over the actions of the party's leaders. Party leaders, in turn, must be willing and able to intervene in administrative matters in support of these groups.[19] Following LaPalombara's analysis we can consider this final component of political structure by asking whether private organizations did in fact become either clients or political kin of agencies responsible for urban renewal and how such relationships in fact conditioned the results of urban renewal in our two cities.

Birmingham before 1972

Birmingham's Comprehensive Redevelopment Program contained two of the principal features that promoted bargaining and policy deflection in British economic policymaking: public and private roles were, in principle, clearly distinguished, and public and private actions had considerable mutual implications for the growth of the city. Nevertheless, negotiations between and among public and private organizations over the substance of redevelopment were, until the advent of the Urban Renewal Program in 1972, infrequent and narrowly delimited.

Just as national economic policy distinguished between industrial sectors that had been nationalized and thus fell under public responsibility and those sectors that remained under private control, Comprehensive Redevelopment essentially divided the city into those neighborhoods under municipal control and those whose development would remain largely a private matter. The fundamental strategy of the program required the city to control investment in declining areas: to purchase all housing considered unfit for habitation, to demolish that housing, and to build municipally owned and managed housing on the cleared land. While politicians may have debated the exact boundaries of the redevelopment areas and the merits of selling municipal houses to tenants, this basic strategy was never seriously questioned before 1972.

Policymakers explicitly rejected cooperative ventures between the city and private property developers. Officials in Birmingham's Public Works and Housing departments never proposed plans that provided investment opportunities for private investors, and politicians never objected. I asked Conservative leaders why no role had been found for private participation in redevelopment. One long-time Tory leader replied, "You'd get a scream if you bought from owner-occupiers and sold to rich developers." Referring to a municipal housing project outside the redevelopment areas, he remarked that "in one scheme, I offered land to builders on the condition we could nominate tenants. But they [private developers] fiddled us on big families, workers, Irishmen, and the like." This man's successor admitted that he would have liked to have included local developers, but "we never advanced private development schemes because we knew they were out of favor." Thus even for the politicians most sympathetic to capitalistic practices, the city and private developers "do not mingle."

Economic planners, as we have seen, bridge this gap between

public and private spheres of influence by promoting and nurturing structures through which various private interests may be represented in policymaking. If the patterns of negotiation and representation that characterize these efforts were translated literally into decision-making patterns for urban renewal, we would find in Birmingham an extensive network of relationships for bargaining over the details of each project. We would expect that the planning and execution of projects that ultimately demolished and rebuilt some 20 percent of a city's housing stock would induce persistent and detailed consultation with a wide range of local individuals and organizations. Such channels would keep policymakers aware of important views concerning the impact of redevelopment and alternatives under consideration for further action. Even ignoring the normative import of functional representation in the British policy process, we would expect urban renewal decision makers to consult, among others, real estate agents and property developers on the implications for the development of the remainder of the city, industrialists and trade unionists on the effects on the city's labor market, major lenders on the impact on the availability of capital for other local investment possibilities, and social and religious organizations on attempts to mitigate the social repercussions of greatly altering the immediate environment of thousands of persons. There are, in addition to these potential client groups, private groups important as constituents of each political party.

I expected to find Birmingham's administrative agencies, especially the Public Works Department, richly supplied with links to the kinds of local organizations just mentioned and thus asked officials to list their most reliable contacts outside the administration for advice and information about urban renewal. Uniformly, these officials failed to understand my question; they failed in particular to understand why they need ever go outside their own agencies for advice. "Our staff is a substantial body thinking for years on these matters," a former deputy chief officer replied. He saw no reason to listen to private sources: "Outsiders may have some fatuous scheme that won't work."

Consultation was only important, he continued, because "ministry inspectors will ask us whom we've talked to." My question troubled this man because he did not trust, and could think of no use for, "outside" opinions.

Other informants were a bit more willing to admit exceptions, but the theme remained the same. A Conservative leader replied: "We have a standing committee with the Chamber of Commerce. For example they're cooperating with us on the National Exhibition Center. We never consult architect, surveyor, or [real] estate agent organizations because they're against us. Maybe an individual, but never the organizations." Similarly, a Public Works official acknowledged that he contacted the Chamber of Commerce or the Chamber of Trades "once every three months on some special issue." These special issues involved matters like the form of the contract given to building tradesmen, rather than the content of policy decisions.

I was able to discover one exception with implications for the substance of the Comprehensive Redevelopment projects. Before redevelopment Birmingham's inner wards were well supplied with small public houses and independent breweries. Redevelopment greatly reduced the number of "locals" and, since pubs are normally tied to a single supplier, raised the issue of which brewer would supply which pub. Consultation among brewers, councillors, and Public Works officials produced a plan assigning pubs to brewers on the basis of preredevelopment barrel sales. The effect of this approach was to favor the few largest breweries to the disadvantage of their smaller competitors. Among the saddest results of redevelopment—attributable to functional representation—was the monopoly given to brewers of pressurized, continuous process beer.

A retired chief officer summarized the role of private organizations in Comprehensive Redevelopment: "Over fifteen to twenty years was there any regular consultation of groups? Answer is, 'No. . . . What's the City Council for?'" Consistently, policymakers considered private organizations as peripheral annoyances; outsiders were rarely seen as either useful allies or potential obstacles to any agency's policy designs. A review of LaPalombara's conditions for *clientela* and *parentela* may show why this unexpected situation developed.

First of all, officials in Birmingham never considered themselves as dependent upon private sources for technical information as economic planners in both Britain and Italy had been. The Public Health, Housing, and Public Works departments considered themselves and one another more trustworthy and reliable than outsiders with "fatuous schemes." Nor did any of these agencies have serious "structural deficencies" that prevented them from performing intelligence duties. In addition neither "value orientations" nor "sociopsychological" needs drew officials into close relations with private groups. Dickensian visions of the slumlord had essentially destroyed the legitimacy of private low-rent housing. A municipal monopoly in this market sector left policymakers with few concerns about future relations with private groups. Finally, the disciplined two-party system could be trusted, officials believed, to "domesticate" the diverse groups interested in urban renewal and to protect officials from the demands these interests might generate.

It follows from this last point and from what we have already seen of the attitudes of leading politicians toward groups within their parties that *parentela* would meet a similar fate. Like the Tory leader who worried that real estate and development groups would oppose municipal programs, Labour Party chairmen and leaders considered themselves free of direct policy pressures from the Birmingham Trades Council and were unwilling to sacrifice administrators' independence to any demands the Trades Council might have wished to make.[20] Again, the Party Groups provided forums for the expression of specific interests, but the groups also authoritatively aggregated those interests into a single party position.

It would be difficult to imagine how, if the implementation of Comprehensive Redevelopment had indeed involved representative patterns like those that characterized economic planning, results so large in compass and complete in plan fulfillment could have been achieved. Crucial to the argument is the fact that the two policies were adopted and carried out in quite different political structures.[21] A strong executive administered Comprehensive Redevelopment in a political context that explicitly delegitimized interested private organizations. The result was a complete takeover by public authorities—it is often called "municipalization"—of urban renewal policy. Unable even to consider complete nationalization of production, economic planners were forced to overlay their sphere of control with a network of functional representation. They were thereby locked into a decision-making process incapable of achieving the level of control reached in urban redevelopment. The public and private sectors remained "utterly distinct" in both cases, but only in urban renewal did government's realm extend to decisions about the most important policy issues.

The most obvious result of this complete takeover was the municipal authorities' high level of control over the projects. The absence of private interference was the final condition allowing Birmingham to redevelop over two decades such large areas with so few significant changes in direction. In addition the substantive results of the programs clearly exhibit the impact of this takeover. Comprehensive Redevelopment was a bureaucrat's program. It entailed clear definitions of subject matter, precise categories of targets, and equal treatment for cases within each category; it provided for strict vertical lines of authority in implementation; and it produced the result best suited to continued administrative control, tracts of municipally owned and managed housing. Give a highly competent group of engineers, architects, public health officers, and housing managers some slums, a lot of capital, and considerable authority, and they will produce Comprehensive Redevelopment.

Birmingham after 1972

Of course, great differences of scope and technique separate the redevelopment of specific neighborhoods of one city—even extensive areas of a very large city—from the management of an advanced, complex economy. The changes in policy and particularly in implementation, however, brought about by the Urban Renewal Program demonstrate that political structures analogous to those conditioning economic planning may be introduced to urban renewal and that analogous institutions may bring analogous results.

Urban Renewal explicitly required substantial private sector participation. The city would provide environmental amenities—small parks, improved streets and sidewalks, increased city services—to Renewal Areas; it would acquire and rejuvenate a small portion of houses itself; and it would provide subsidies to home owners who wished to rehabilitate their own homes. In contrast to Comprehensive Redevelopment, however, Urban Renewal depended on individual, private decisions to accept these incentives and subsidies and invest in substantially deteriorated houses. While the politicians who conceived Urban Renewal believed that they had stacked the cards in favor of home owners who decided to invest, the problem remained of convincing enough individuals and organizing sufficient efforts to create a unified program. How are piecemeal decisions to be controlled? The original problem returns.

Extensive consultation between the municipal agencies involved in Urban Renewal and private groups concerned with the rehabilitation of inner-city housing became the solution to the problem of control. As with Comprehensive Redevelopment, the list of groups could have been quite long; it was not. The authors of Urban Renewal could have coordinated public and private action by entering into agreements with a few firms large enough to finance and manage the rebuilding of large segments of the Renewal Areas. Or, the city's administration could have been enlarged sufficiently to permit individual contact with the thousands of tenants and home owners in Renewal Areas—most British cities followed this course. Instead, the Urban Renewal Conference chose to limit consultation to groups considered to represent tenants and home owners in the Renewal Areas. This course of action was not accidental; it resulted from the substantial political changes Birmingham experienced between 1966 and 1972.

As we have already seen, Labour councillors elected in the early 1970s had developed and nurtured unusually strong ties with individuals and groups within their wards. As these same councillors began to consider means for redirecting the city's urban renewal efforts, these neighborhood ties had a powerful influence on their efforts. Each of the three major components of the new approach—direct public participation, reorganized administration, and emphasis on building retention and improvement—felt the impact of this influence.

"A week after I became a councillor," one of the early advocates of housing retention and rehabilitation told me, "I held the first public meeting ever in Saint James," an area included in the second phase of Comprehensive Redevelopment. His initial goals, he claimed, dealt with public relations and information: "Keep up stability and confidence." In redevelopment areas, he remembered thinking, "Inhabitants don't understand the local authority's problems." Public meetings, however, revealed a level of hostility surprising even to the newly elected representative. He found many "mainly local groups were starting up. They were becoming a real opposition force, which we thought was the wrong approach, and we wanted to put our case before them to get their confidence." It was out of these contacts with often-hostile neighborhood groups that public participation grew to be a major component of the Urban Renewal Program.

Two aspects of this push toward participation are particularly revealing. First, advocates of the altered policy sought not only to deal with and co-opt existing groups but to stimulate the growth of organized community groups where none existed. The Urban Renewal Conference's first chairman reported contacting all the groups he could find. "I told groups that existed to send representatives to a liaison committee and tried to encourage groups to form in other areas. . . . No one could say they weren't consulted." And yet this extensive view of participation did not extend to interests other than those of home owners and tenants. When I asked the same man about contacts with commercial and industrial firms in the Renewal Areas, he became as puzzled as his predecessors had been when I raised the topic of consultation. To questions about contacts with industrialists he replied, "They didn't live there; they weren't interested in the areas." Considering shopkeepers, he admitted, "Some are residents. We did nothing directly to help commerce. No problem of shops closing down; not that's been brought to my attention at least. Other things came first." Legitimacy had indeed been extended to private groups, but the extent of that legitimacy was narrowly confined.

Relations between community group leaders and the administrators of Urban Renewal demonstrate that this grant of legitimacy produced real changes in the policymaking process. A Housing Department official with responsibilities for Urban Renewal admitted that "consultation was a new thing—officers are anything but one with it." When, however, I asked him to list useful private sources of information he quickly named several community groups and their leaders whom he contacted frequently and informally. These groups, he reported, supplied important advice and information on a variety of topics related to Urban Renewal. Similarly, the organizer of a community group helping to manage one Renewal Area remarked that he knew of some thirty-five or forty groups like his own. Before Urban Renewal "you could count them on one hand." A remarkable change in the role of functional representation indeed characterized Urban Renewal.

A wide variety of actual practices, not to mention flagrant shams, has been called public participation in public policymaking.[22] Urban Renewal aimed at an extreme by delegating substantial responsibility for the rehabilitation of designated communities to representatives of those communities. In principle the council agreed to buy and rehabilitate the remainder of homes in a given block if the owners of at least 80 percent agreed to accept grants, invest personal funds, and rehabilitate their houses. In practice this level of agreement could only be achieved with the cooperation of indigenous organizers able to work out agreements between home owners who might be willing to risk improving their homes and the city, which could offer varying amounts of incentives to investors.

The implementation of Urban Renewal thus became a problem of negotiation, and the overall strategy included administrative changes designed to facilitate bargaining. Once the council adopted Urban Renewal in 1972, an urban renewal officer was appointed and assigned to designated teams of officials for each Renewal Area.[23] The members of these project teams came from each of the municipal departments concerned with urban renewal—Housing, Public Works, Health, City Architect's—and remained employees of that department.

The teams' responsibilities were twofold. First, they were supposed to coordinate, at the neighborhood level, the efforts of their respective departments. Second, team members were to be the meeting point between municipal authority and local participation. "I wanted to get officers out working in the community," said the Urban Renewal Conference chairman. "'Get them on your side,' I'd tell the project teams." The Public Works Department sat astride Comprehensive Redevelopment and held its reins firmly; management strategies for Urban Renewal simultaneously broke this dominance and brought community representatives directly into the process of policymaking.

In short, Urban Renewal brought Birmingham a structure for relationships between public and private organizations that greatly altered existing practices. The new structure introduced patterns of consultation and dependence on private organizations similar to those that had characterized national economic policies. An important contrast, however, must be noted. While consultation on economic policy grew out of the needs and beliefs of the administration, community participation in Urban Renewal was imposed by the Labour majority in the city council. Community groups gained access to Urban Renewal decision making because these groups were or could be adopted as *parenti* of the local Labour Party. The revised political structure provided conditions for *parentela* almost as explicitly as its predecessor had locked out *clientela*.

Three of LaPalombara's four conditions for *parentela* clearly existed after the Labour Party's return to council control in 1972. From that point, "bureaucrats perceived the dominant party as willing to intervene in the administrative process on behalf of its own narrow interests, or those of groups affiliated with the party."[24] Officials who had worked with and supported Comprehensive Redevelopment consistently complained to me of increased interference by politicians in the details of their work. Some of these men attributed failures to receive promotions to their admitted reluctance to work closely with the younger politicians and the community groups; others used the reorganization of local government in 1974 as a convenient moment to retire. For their part, younger Labour Party leaders stressed their desire to involve themselves and their community group allies in the details of administering Urban Renewal. One of these leaders admitted that recent chief officer appointees had been brought to Birmingham from other cities because outsiders would be less difficult to dominate. He went on to lament his inability to apply explicitly partisan criteria to professional appointments. Politicians had become willing to "politicize" administration, and bureaucrats, of course, recognized the change.

The next condition LaPalombara lists for *parentela* is the group's "capacity to condition the party,"[25] especially through an ability to control votes.[26] Although it would be impossible, with existing data, to estimate the number of votes actually influenced by community organizations, patterns of voting in British municipal elections indicate that the number may well have been rather small. The important point remains, however, that politicians considered these votes crucial to victory. As we have already seen, Labour Party leaders attributed electoral losses in the late 1960s to their having paid insufficient attention to neighborhoods included in Comprehensive Redevelopment, just as they attributed later victories to improved contacts with groups and individuals in these areas. A Labour leader, first elected in

1970, tersely summarized the basic issue: retention and participation were, he said, "not political but humanitarian for me. But it was clear that if we did nothing we'd be in trouble politically." Whatever their real electoral value, community groups had gained leverage within the Labour Party.

Finally, LaPalombara argues, *parentela* groups "thrive in administrative situations that are muddy and confused."[27] While the administration of Urban Renewal hardly approached the level of confusion LaPalombara found in parts of the Italian bureaucracy, the firm hierarchy and clear lines of authority of Comprehensive Redevelopment had surely softened and blurred. Delegation of authority to project teams in Renewal Areas, shared responsibilities for projects, and direct community participation were adopted precisely to increase the permeability of decision-making structures and to avoid the kind of dominance the Public Works Department held over Comprehensive Redevelopment. As LaPalombara predicts, this blurring of authority was an invitation to increased interest group access.

LaPalombara advances a fourth condition for successful *parentela*; in fact he calls it the "key variable affecting *parentela*": the hegemonic quality of the party.[28] Where no one party promises to dominate political conflict indefinitely, bureaucrats enjoy greater freedom of action and can resist partisan attempts to impose *parentela* groups upon them. Birmingham clearly does not meet this condition. The regular alternation of parties in control of the city council must have led all participants to anticipate an eventual end to the sponsorship community groups enjoyed under Labour control. We may speculate that recognition of this eventuality led Urban Renewal advocates to take great care in chief officer appointments and administrative reorganization to ensure that community participation became firmly entrenched. Only if community groups succeeded in a metamorphosis from *parentela to clientela* groups—from partnership with the Labour Party to partnership with the local bureaucracy—could this remarkable form of consultation be expected to survive Labour's loss of control, which occurred in 1976.

By 1972, then, national and local political leaders were aligned behind an approach to urban renewal that stressed the retention and rehabilitation of existing structures and slowed the process of replacing inadequate housing. A low level of physical change followed as a consequence. Political forces particular to Birmingham, however, had further implications for the results this new approach would achieve. The requirements for consultation and participation were perhaps the most important political determinant of the content of the Urban Renewal Program. In particular the high level of control that had been such a striking characteristic of Comprehensive Redevelopment was greatly reduced.

The reason for this important change in urban renewal policy lies in these efforts to incorporate private groups into the planning and execution of the program. No longer could any single agency decide and manage both the outline and the details of an overall, comprehensive urban renewal plan. Instead the program depended upon the assent and cooperation of a large number of groups and individuals. Because these new participants often had a quite limited scope of concern (as limited as one row house), it is not surprising that the scope of decisions narrowed as well. Where Comprehensive Redevelopment plans could be imposed by the hundreds of acres, Urban Renewal plans had to be negotiated by the terrace. A much lower level of policy control, of course, resulted.

Juxtaposed, Comprehensive Redevelopment and Urban Renewal illustrate the structure of public-private relations in British urban planning, two variations of that structure, and its consequences for the substance of public policy. In both programs public and private did, in fact, remain distinct. In the former, Redevelopment Areas were wholly public concerns; there simply was no room for private involvement. The structural change with Urban Renewal was the recognition of owner-occupiers as legitimate, independent private actors. Private involvement became crucial to the realization of public goals, but remained an independent sphere of action. As with economic planning, an extensive network of consultation bridged the public-private gap, and as with economic planning, the compass of public action shrank appreciably.

Lyon

In contrast to government officials in Birmingham, officials in Lyon were systematically dependent on the cooperation of private groups. This dependence, surprising in light of the high level of autonomy attributed to the French government in its attempts to direct the economy, profoundly shaped the extent and results of the city's urban renewal efforts. The solution to this puzzle lies in an understanding relationship between the agencies responsible for urban renewal and private developers and builders that is quite unlike the relationship Shonfield, Hayward, and Suleiman describe.

French administrative and political officials have considered urban development and redevelopment as processes similar to economic planning, that is, as ones demanding shared public and private responsibility. Illustrative of this viewpoint is a 1970 Ministère de l'Equipement and du logement circular:

> If the new industrially based society is heralded by urban concentrations, it must also be characterized by a way of life and an environment fit to satisfy the collective needs that every day are greater.
> To put in place the means to face up to that demand is the imperative duty of the government and especially the Ministère de l'Equipement which is responsible for urban planning. . . .
> Beyond that point it would be in vain and dangerous: —to wish in the name of order to undertake a restrictive or purely administrative approach to urban planning that would amount to a denial of an ineluctable phenomenon—or to wish to direct it [urbanization] *without joining together all the country's economic agents.* [29]

The goal of urban planning so considered is, in Shonfield's terms, "to secure a general bias" in patterns of urban development, whoever undertakes significant projects.

The key term for describing this approach is *"urbanisme op-erationnel."* This phrase signifies an approach to planning that is neither limited to regulative private initiatives nor extended to full public takeover of urban development. It includes on the one hand planning by projects or zones that "benefit from a cer-tain autonomy of conception and execution in relation to the sur-rounding metropolitan area,"[30] and on the other, direct, goal-oriented intervention by *both* public and private actors. Once again, reaching collective goals for development demands *con-certation*: concerted public and private efforts. The Urban Com-mission for the Sixth Plan argued that urban planning was less a matter of "constructing [regulatory] plans than imagining and defining goals . . . and elaborating processes to attain them." These processes, according to the commission, must include the "diverse agents" who might sponsor "spontaneous development" and must see that their efforts conform to the "objectives of the metropolitan area."[31]

In achieving *"urbanisme operationnel,"* however, private de-velopers' "concerted action [*concertation*] with the public agen-cies, going as far in certain cases as contractual arrangements, is one of the methods that can be used most efficaciously."[32] Cities should reach their development goals, in other words, not by setting regulations and waiting for private action, and not, we may infer, by doing large amounts of their own building, but by engaging and directing the energy and capital of the private sector.

An urban planner, who directed urban renewal in Villefranche-sur-Saône, explains the role of *concertation* in redevelopment efforts:

It thus clearly appears that public powers ought to intervene [in urban renewal] both to make the project compulsory and to permit it to break even financially. Such an intervention places urban re-newal in its "public" framework within which actions dominated by private interests are pursued. Thus the two-headed character of this form of operational urban planning, which has some public objectives and which must therefore be integrated in a "program" relevant to a planned economy, but which is only realized as the sum of private actions that remain in the framework of the free market clearly appears.[33]

Urban renewal, like economic and other cases of urban planning, depends jointly on the state's ability and willingness to set a course of action authoritatively and on private investors' ability and willingness to follow where governmentally provided opportunities lead. Private actions may be individually determined and profit motivated, but they will not be piecemeal because the state will ensure that they adhere to a common plan.

In Lyon, two very different projects illustrate the potential and limitations of urban renewal by *concertation*. Public and semipublic agencies conceived and designed both the Part-Dieu and the Place Forez projects; both depended, however, on private investment to reach fruition.

It would be difficult to find a better example of *concertation* in urban planning than the redevelopment of the Part-Dieu. The entire concept of the project depended jointly on the municipal and central governments' abilities to obtain urban land and plan for its use and on the interest of investors in supplying expensive commercial and office buildings to the local property market. As the undertaking evolved from a low-income housing project, controlled by the local housing authority, to a new city center for the growing metropolis, the role played by public-private collaboration became increasingly decisive for the content of the project and potentially for the development of the left bank of the Rhone.

The key to the political process that motivated this evolution and produced the Part-Dieu project was the Société d'Equipement de la région lyonnaise. We have already seen the important role this semipublic corporation played in providing working capital for and facilitating Parisian intervention in local public works projects. An additional source of the S E R L's power is implicit in its juridical category. As a *société d'économie mixte*, it can, as a senior S E R L official put it, "play the game on both sides [*jouer l'amalgame*]."

Like a private business, it can buy, sell, contract, and litigate. In doing so the mixed corporation is free from the rigid constraints that administrative law would place on local governments. Yet municipal and departmental councils nominate a majority of the corporation's directors and may delegate to it certain municipal powers, notably the authority to acquire land by condemnation. Independently assured of financial and technical resources, corporations like the SERL incarnate *concertation*.

In principle the SERL simply plays the middleman's role in urban renewal. In the name of the municipality it buys the designated land, clears existing buildings, replaces streets, sewers, and other elements of infrastructure, and sells parcels of cleared land to the government agencies, private developers, and public authorities that will rebuild the redeveloped sector. In principle, again, all of this buying, equipping, and selling is done in accordance with plans that the ministerial and municipal technical services develop and the municipal council approves.

The hitch, which significantly enhances the SERL's importance, is that buying and equipping are very expensive and cannot safely take place until selling—at a favorable price—is reasonably well assured.[34] That assurance can only come from extensive, detailed consultation and negotiation between planners and potential users. Such contacts serve to elicit information about the demand for land and infrastructure and about mutually acceptable mixes of land use after renewal. Furthermore, because public users with a large demand for urban land (primarily the municipal housing corporations) face low statutory ceilings on the prices they can pay for building land, private builders are the critical second party to these consultations.[35] Negotiation with the office and commercial developers whose buildings came to dominate the Part-Dieu was, according the officials both of the SERL and of central and municipal governments, virtually the exclusive province of the SERL.

The SERL's project director for the Part-Dieu explained the course taken by these negotiations. Essentially, he argued, the corporation enabled the city "to engage in land speculation and make developers pay for new public facilities" in return for providing lucrative investment opportunities. Public intervention in the aging industrial areas of the left bank had driven the value of land acquired from the army from 30 million (new) francs in 1960 to (he estimated) 60 or 70 million by 1975. The sale of part of this land to private developers at these inflated prices covered not only acquisition, clearance, and public works expenses, but would, according to the DDE official most directly concerned with the project, produce a surplus.

The result was much what we would expect of French planning efforts: public and private action were tightly entwined. Public authority aggregated investment decisions for a fairly extensive area of the city and thus created conditions conducive to substantial private investment in urban redevelopment. There was, however, a price to be paid. The voice of any public authority in determining the direction these investments would take or what would be built, was strikingly small. Again, the role played by the SERL illustrates the trades and compromises involved.

The project director quite explicitly recognized that negotiation and budget balancing rather than holistic, purposive planning, were the SERL's forte. "At the SERL we know how to manage things very well. But for reflective city planning, that's not us. . . . but we know how to run things like a private concern, although we're not interested in profit." Thus, SERL officials conducted an international search for investors that attracted Swiss and British department stores and British property developers, as well as the major French banks and property developers, to build a one-million-square-foot shopping mall, four large private office buildings, and a luxury hotel. The project director could not help agreeing with his leftist critics who protested that the area had been "colonized."

One claim of this gentleman must be questioned: that the SERL has no interest in profit. Although the SERL's managers have no dividend-hungry stockholders to confront, strong incentives to realize a financial gain do exist. First of all, the SCET's continuing support is crucial to the corporation's survival, but that support may weaken in the face of repeated deficits. A sen-

ior SERL official cited mixed corporations that had suffered
such a fate. Second, financial surpluses from any one project
may be transferred to any other SERL project and increase flex-
ibility of action in the latter case. Third, the SERL receives a
percentage of the transactions it manages for "its own expenses."
Obviously, the more costly the projects undertaken, the more
money that is available for development and expansion of the
corporation. Finally, the Lyon city administration has been unwilling to subsidize money-losing projects. A SCET official
stated flatly: "In the absence of a clear policy to the contrary, the
mixed corporation will act to reduce municipal financial participation." Lyon never adopted a policy to the contrary.[36] As a
result of these internal and external financial pressures, SERL
officials steered the development of the Part-Dieu toward ever-
increasing gains from land sales.

The most important and most illustrative tack used to increase
land values within the Part-Dieu project was the stimulation of
Lyon's office market. Until the late 1960s, converted residential
buildings provided the bulk of Lyon's corporate and professional
office space; additional conversions of stately Presqu'île apartments satisfied expanding demand. Recognizing a potential market for new, purposely built office space, SERL officials attempted to interest local developers in the use of Part-Dieu land
for new office construction—at land prices considerably above
those to be paid for residential developments. "No one would
believe us," reported a SERL official, who complained of the
conservative Lyonnais business community; a private developer
could not be found. As a result, the SERL, with financial and
technical support from the SCET,[37] took the unusual step of financing, building, and promoting a large, modern office building within the Part-Dieu project without a private partner. Before plans for the SERL were complete, every available office
had been rented. With the demand demonstrated, the SERL
experienced little difficulty in selling three additional parcels of
land to French and British development corporations and a private French bank for the construction of a total of two million

square feet of office space. These sales were major factors in the financial surplus expected from the Part-Dieu project.

The S E R L's promotion of office construction makes clear the meaning of the project director when he contrasted "reflective urban planning," which the S E R L could not do, with the "management" of development, which it did quite well. The level of control over development that directors of Birmingham's Comprehensive Redevelopment Program or even its Urban Renewal Program exercised was impossible to achieve when the final decision to build or not to build lay with private, individual promoters. For the Part-Dieu the same agency simply did not have the jurisdiction that the Public Works Department had in the Birmingham projects. Moreover, control as I have defined it had to be lower in Lyon where final decisions were always subject to market conditions at the time they were made. Indeed public agencies could affect the real estate market in major ways, but they remained subject to its general principles and limited by considerations resembling profitability. As a S E R L economist put it, "What we do is provide a little constraint for the private market." Providing constraint, however, implies that an important motive force lay elsewhere.

Although very different in both methods and goals, the Place Forez project, which was contemporary with the Part-Dieu project, illustrates just as clearly the pivotal position of private investment in urban renewal by *concertation*. With much more modest goals than those for the Part-Dieu, the Place Forez project set out to induce the owners of twenty-nine deteriorating apartment buildings in that sector of the Croix-Rousse area to provide structural improvements and basic amenities for their buildings. As with the Part-Dieu, public agencies provided technical and design assistance and helped to arrange financing, but the decision whether to renovate remained in private hands. Unlike the Part-Dieu project, in the Place Forez project ownership and, it was hoped, tenancy would remain unaltered. The provision of free design assistance, partial government grants, and subsidized loans would presumably make resulting rent increases minimal.[38]

Again the state's chief role lies in dominating piecemeal change. As we saw in Chapter 1, among important factors inhibiting the improvement of housing in deteriorating neighborhoods is the concern that one's own investment will yield an acceptable return only if neighboring buildings are similarly improved. To surmount this problem, legislation providing subsidies to projects like the Place Forez required the municipal council to declare that buildings not improved by their owners would be acquired and improved by the city. Thus in late 1968 and early 1969 after a lengthy series of largely informational and, according to the project's director, pro forma hearings, owners of all residential properties in the Place Forez sector received letters from the mayor of Lyon instructing them either to fulfill a schedule of improvements or to sell their buildings. The letters served a dual purpose, of course; owners were not only officially notified of required repairs but simultaneously assured that owners of adjoining buildings faced similar requirements.

For the Place Forez project the actual work of *concertation*— negotiating improvement schedules for specific buildings, arranging financing, seeking municipal action—was entrusted to the Association de Restauration immobilière.[39] Juridically a voluntary organization, the ARIM served as intermediary between central and municipal government agencies and owners of the designated buildings, a role comparable to that of the SERL in the Part-Dieu, Moncey Nord, and Martinière-Tolozan projects. In contrast to the SERL, however, the ARIM lacked access to an independent source of capital and thus could not itself buy or renovate buildings in the renewal area.

This lack of independence was a crucial factor in the project's rather mediocre outcome. No means existed to compel owners who agreed to undertake improvements to adhere to ARIM plans or to ensure their cooperation in providing evironmental amenities.[40] Worse yet, buildings whose owners refused to cooperate were simply allowed to decay. "Two of the buildings," the ARIM director reported, "were demolished by the city, but there were another seven where the owners decided to sell, but no one would buy. We managed to get state aid to buy one of them, but for the others, no one has bought them, and the work's never been done. Now they're in deplorable condition." Faced with such unhappy consequences, the ARIM had no choice other than to allow willing landlords to dictate their own terms and conditions for the work actually undertaken.

The ARIM director blamed his lack of working capital, and thus his dependence upon landlords' access to capital, for the lack of control and limited results achieved in the Place Forez project. He expressed greater hopes for the association's second restoration project, then just beginning. This project had the more modest aim of preventing the physical decline of a still rather elegant neighborhood near the city's central square. The greater prosperity of the residents, the higher level of owner-occupied (co-op) apartments, and the greater potential market for its housing made the chances for success in the later project seem greater. And yet these very conditions for success demonstrate how far this kind of project is removed from publicly controlled redevelopment of deteriorated urban areas.

If urban renewal in Birmingham consisted of bureaucrats' projects and politicians' projects, urban renewal in Lyon was land developers' projects. Discussions with planners, developers, community organizers, and politicians left no phrase as firmly etched in my mind as *"le prix des terrains"*—the price of land. The prices for which urban land could be bought and sold consistently and profoundly affected the extent and character of urban renewal in Lyon. Areas of the city in which *no* urban renewal occurred demonstrate this point as clearly as do the characteristics of those projects actually undertaken. The Courly's commissioner of public works pointed to numerous areas of the Croix-Rousse in need of intervention to reduce densities and clear blight. "We won't do much in the Croix-Rousse," he said. "It doesn't interest the developers. The work is too expensive."

Perhaps this gentleman too easily dismissed local political constraints, but he blamed the city's failure to do more aggressive renewal and particularly its failure to provide low-income housing in previous projects on the city's lack of control over building land. He envied English municipal authorities, he said. "In England the cities are landlords—no problems, no expropriation. They can provide public facilities." While this informant may have overestimated the extent of British municipalization, he did identify precisely one of the principal institutional factors that make him a much weaker policymaker than his former counterpart in Birmingham.

This weakness stands out even more clearly if we recall that only one of Lyon's projects (the Grande Côte) did not start from a parcel of land made available by some external event or decision. The DDE official responsible for urban development projects contrasted the Grande-Rue de la Croix-Rousse, a potential renewal site, with the Part-Dieu. In the former case, a densely populated, heavily commercial area, costs of land acquisition and housing would prohibit urban renewal, however valuable such an effort might potentially be. The latter, because it contained an obsolete military installation, was "an excellent opportunity. In the 1960s," he observed, "there was a disposition toward renovation, and projects were previewed on paper. However, the city and the SERL have searched out the areas where success was easiest."[41]

The record bears out this observation. Moncey Nord centered around a large, charity geriatrics home, closed and donated to the city; Martinière-Tolozan first sat on the shoulders of an expressway project and later on those of the metro; and Place Forez resulted from a specific, experimental government program.[42] For most parts of Lyon the *prix des terrains* prevented direct public attempts to redirect the course of development or decay.

Where urban renewal did, in fact, take place, another of its consequences can be traced to *concertation*: in each project, except Place Forez and Martinière-Tolozan, where little change of any sort took place, the social character of the renewed area changed drastically. Boury summarizes the dilemma that led numerous French cities to this result:

> If construction of social [welfare] character [i.e., low-income housing and facilities to serve it] is desired, the renewal agency must set land prices that do not exceed a certain ceiling price; for unregulated construction, prices are simply based on the local market. The choice between these different types of construction poses the fundamental problem of urban renewal. . . . Whatever [the theoretical principles] may be, by the force of things the renewal agency will seek to obtain the maximum return from the resale of land, on the one hand to save public money but also—when in the presence of private constructors—because it seems preferable to make the cleared lands pay as well as possible rather than permit developers to benefit from increased land values.[43]

We have already seen this logic played out in the Part-Dieu project. In a similar way Moncey Nord changed from a low to a high-income neighborhood. Informants consistently acknowledged that to the extent that urban renewal was carried out, Martinière-Tolozan would eventually undergo a similar transformation although sitting tenants might be protected. In fact, long-range central government planners, arguing that Lyon required considerable inner-city residential redevelopment, observed, "Housing, of considerable variety, must be the object of a very large redevelopment effort. The number of inhabitants will not change greatly, but the social groups residing in the urban core will be modified by the effects of redevelopment and the increases of rents."[44] Because *concertation* ties urban renewal to the pursuit of profit and the local property market, it must result in significant social change. Uses more profitable than low-income housing may always be found for cleared, well located city-center land.

Some French scholars have argued that this pattern of social change is less an unavoidable outcome than a calculated goal of urban redevelopment. Looking also at Lyon, Jean Lojkine has argued that social change and "deindustrialization" were explicit goals of urban renewal. The programs were essentially the "enterprise of systematic eviction from the city of productive activities"[45] and of the people who worked in them. As a result, "urban policy has accelerated the objective processes of social polarization"[46] associated with the international monopoly phase of capitalism. In a study of urban redevelopment in Paris, Manuel Castells has put the argument more forcefully. Urban renewal, the "Reconquest of Paris" was "an offensive on the part of the dominant class"[47] to achieve the "reproduction of the urban system of the Paris region, from the point of view of its centrality, at the higher level of the productive apparatus and of urban stratification."[48] At the same time the projects served to consolidate the Gaullist majority's control of Parisian politics.[49] All of this follows the "spatial logic of the most dynamic sectors of international monopoly capitalism."[50]

These arguments are compelling as descriptions of an urban renewal strategy that would appeal to those in government and private enterprise who had the most to gain from high-level tertiary development, increasing urban land values, and conservative politics. The analysis has, however, major shortcomings in its ability to explain the outcomes of urban renewal programs. In particular, Castells and Lojkine do not provide for variation in monopoly capital's success in realizing this strategy. Lojkine reports that in Lyon the coherent deindustrialization program is in practice "piecemeal [*ponctuelle*], discontinuous."[51] In contrast the Parisian program appears from Castells's account to have been more completely executed. Why would this "unconscious logic" of the dominant class be more fully realized in one French city than in another? The answer apparently lies in the day-to-day politics of policy implementation, a matter for which the Marxist concern for global tendencies leaves little room.[52]

This point is made even more clearly by contrasting the programs in both Lyon and Paris with those in Birmingham where the social content of urban redevelopment was just the opposite. Urban renewal programs in Birmingham *confirmed* the hold—

albeit at lower densities—of working-class residents on central city areas. Yet Great Britain is presumably at a stage of capitalist development similar to that of France. Although no one would argue that the logic of international monopoly capital should explain everything about urban policymaking, the contrasts between Lyon and Birmingham do pose serious problems for the Marxist analysis. Some missing element accounts for the great differences in the extent to which class interests were translated into urban policy in the two cities.

I have argued that differences in the structure of public-private relations in the two cities provide this missing connection. Freed of the need to attract private investment, officials in Birmingham were also freed of the need to respond to private locational preferences. Consequently the social welfare content of Birmingham's central city renewal program was preserved although the diversion of British capital to French urban renewal projects like the Part-Dieu may have been a further consequence of the same freedom.

A third consequence of public-private relationships for Lyon's urban renewal projects further clarifies the origins of a previously noted characteristic: a low level of policy control. The point scarcely needs elaboration. The final content of each project depended on continuing negotiations among a mix of public and private actors over actions each would take. Over the course of these negotiations money and property markets changed, and past commitments weakened. A holistic view of any project was consequently mere fantasy. The Part-Dieu project director's self-characterization as a "manager" rather than a "reflective" city planner was a recognition of just how much or how little policy control public agencies could achieve over urban renewal carried out under these political conditions. As the director himself pointed out, the finished product resulted more from many relatively independent decisions than from an overall plan: "There never was a plan for rebuilding, never a plan for the ensemble. . . . There was no opportunity for programming the projects, for planning the investments." The Part-Dieu was not unique in this respect—only bigger. Public money and authority could be used in these projects to set a new course for development and provide "constraint for the free market," but public agencies were not, as they were in Birmingham, the decisive factor in determining the results.

These three consequences of relationships between the public and private organizations concerned with Lyon's urban renewal—the limited scope of possible projects, the amount of social change that resulted, and the lack of policy control achieved in the projects' implementation—suggest that *concertation*, as we have considered it so far, may be seriously flawed as a strategy for overcoming piecemeal change in urban development. Instead of generating private capital to fulfill *public* development plans, the view students of economic planning have taken, public planning agencies repeatedly adapt their goals for urban renewal to the needs of *private* investors. *Concertation*, it would seem, denotes a species of relationships in which public and private power are not "utterly distinct" and are able to "mingle." Such relationships, however, may vary considerably, with different distributions of power having quite different consequences for public policy. The form of *concertation* prevalent in Lyon's urban renewal projects combined a rather weak public sector with considerable private influence; *concertation* had become *clientela*.

LaPalombara writes: "The *clientela* relationship exists when an interest group, for whatever reasons, succeeds in becoming, in the eyes of a given administrative agency, the natural expression and representative of a given social sector which, in turn, constitutes the natural target or reference point for the activity of the administrative agency."[53] Lyon's actual and potential landowners and developers achieved just such a relationship. The agencies responsible for implementing urban renewal came to depend on these private owners and investors as the source for reviving those parts of the city under their charge.

If we substitute capital for information in LaPalombara's list of variables conditioning the development of *clientela*, we can see how this dependence came about. *Clientela* can develop, LaPalombara argues, when administrative agencies must deal with private groups toward which the administrators are largely sympathetic and from which they require the information to make their work possible. Similarly, officials of the SERL and the ARIM saw investors, builders, and landlords as crucial to the accomplishment of their own work. These private groups stood in need of "domestication," to be sure, but as long as private groups had access to building capital and the public (or semi-public) agencies did not, the former's views about the amount, location, and content of urban renewal would remain a major determinant in Lyon's policymaking.

If observers are correct in arguing that French economic planners consult or ignore private groups and firms almost at will, then Lyon's urban planners occupy a very different political position. The "French model" of "indicative" planning applies poorly to urban renewal. The financial indispensability of landlords and property developers assured these private groups access to decisions about Lyon's urban renewal program, whatever the wishes of public planners may have been. It was clear to all that these investors could and would withhold means crucial to a project's accomplishment unless that project advanced their own interests. No other course would be consistent with the pursuit of profit. Thus while public and private organizations may have cooperatively undertaken urban renewal in Lyon, public agencies simply lacked the political and economic muscle to insist that projects fulfill a publicly imposed plan.

As with Birmingham's Urban Renewal Program, public-private relations became a major factor in a low level of plan fulfillment in Lyon. Unlike either Birmingham program, however, Lyon's pattern of *concertation* also produced considerable social change in renewal areas. The need to provide profitable investment opportunities made low-income housing an all but impossible component of the restructured neighborhoods. Private groups may have been important in both cases, but the interests the groups insisted upon protecting differed vastly.

When governments commit their authority and resources to urban renewal, they are, as we have seen throughout this study, attempting to structure and direct the way the city changes, to make that change purposive and coherent rather than piecemeal. Governmental intervention, however, is no guarantee that coherent results will finally be achieved. The degree to which government agencies are able to dominate interested private groups is as much a political matter as the ability of these agencies to dominate one another. Where agencies, like the Birmingham Public Works Department, can create and implement renewal plans without reliance upon the support, advice, or active cooperation of private groups, coherent single-minded programs are likely to result. To the extent, however, that these private groups become crucial to the accomplishment of any renewal effort, the decision and implementation process becomes more open to more diverse negotiation and comes to resemble more closely the free market. Piecemeal change, albeit change that might otherwise never have occurred, once again comes to characterize urban renewal.

Urban Revival   5

Beyond the Synoptic Ideal

We began this excursion into the implementation of urban redevelopment programs in Lyon and Birmingham in pursuit of a
policymaking ideal and the political conditions that could translate that ideal into practice. We have learned that aspirations
and even carefully coordinated plans do not themselves produce
synoptic policymaking. Instead such plans and aspirations confront political systems varyingly amenable to holistic approaches
to complex social issues. The result is that tightly drawn designs
for urban revival begin to resemble jigsaw puzzles made of pre-
cut pieces of public policy. As the puzzle's assembly proceeds,
the original design often disappears. Politics often enables actors
to reshape pieces to their liking or to withhold them entirely.
Sometimes an unexpected picture emerges, sometimes several
pictures, sometimes no picture at all.

The frequent failure of implementation, the slip between aspiration and realization, is not necessarily the result of unsystematic planning. Governments—all of them, though to varying
extents—must satisfy a mix of groups and individuals that do the
state's bidding and sustain its authority. In so doing, responsible
officials must constantly make and allow others to make decisions that fit poorly with plans the same officials may earlier have
embraced. Consequently, governments rarely act like collective
personalities, and even if they did, they might change their collective minds in the middle of a program. As two Americans ob-
serve, "The national motto, *E pluribus unum*, simply does not
apply to relations among Federal agencies."[1] Federal agencies
are not unique in this respect.

Again, the political forces that push governments away from
synoptic action vary in their intensity from time to time and

from place to place. Examples of relatively systematic and coherent policymaking do exist. To understand the political conditions that underlie this variation is to be able, with a certain level of confidence, to estimate the likelihood that specific governments can achieve these relatively high levels of coordination. To make such estimates is then to suggest just how sensible a given approach to collective problem solving may be in a given time and place.

Urban renewal programs are particularly useful in revealing these political conditions because they assume that public policy can be made highly synoptically. Note, for example, Birmingham's former chief public works officer's view of how urban renewal should be practiced: "The main thing is to have a program, flexible in minor detail, but clearly to be followed once it has been established that overall arguments for it at any stage, outweigh the disadvantages considered from a particular aspect."[2] Implicit in the strategy of urban renewal, this emphasis on synopsis is fundamental to the kind of change that such programs aim to bring about.

Reasons for this approach are easily found. The strategy that underlies urban renewal recognizes that private action is atomistic. Individual responses to perceived market forces are the major factor in determining what will be built where and when. These individual responses add up to patterns of urbanization, but do not necessarily add up to urbanized results that the collectivity might prefer given the opportunity to view urban change holistically.

In particular, market forces will not impel private actors to take risks that (1) hinge upon the coordinate action of other individuals but that having been taken (2) *decrease* the probability that those coordinate actions will in fact occur. Only the application of public authority, so the strategy proceeds, can force the reliably coordinated actions that serve the general welfare. The government—to return to the famous Prisoners' Dilemma—holds the tongue of both captives.[3]

Although this strategy correctly sees private, market-driven action as atomistic, the implied view of governmental action as cohesive and unified does not survive close scrutiny. Birmingham's and Lyon's experience with urban renewal demonstrates the danger in assuming that governmental authority can be applied (by an unnamed subject) in support of a coordinated, carefully packaged urbanization policy. This experience likewise suggests problems with assuming that governmental action will necessarily systematically translate the interests of any given social group or class into tangible results. Government was not necessarily the agent of either ruling-class domination or greater social equality, although those with other forms of social power like capital were best able to constrain governmental action. While governmental assumption of major responsibility for the cities' development did reduce the number of actors whose investment decisions were important to that development, in neither case was that number permanently reduced to one. Instead, governmental intervention resulted in considerable variation in the number of persons and organizations making decisions important to the substance of urban renewal projects and therefore considerable variation in the degree to which the synoptic strategy fit political reality.

While we must be cautious in generalizing from a few urban renewal projects to all spheres of public policy, we can follow these examples to a more realistic view of governance in liberal societies. The singleness of purpose with which public authority is exercised is a variable quantity. If we cease, therefore, to think of "the government" as one collective personality and begin to consider the plurality of agencies and individuals responsible for the exercise of governmental authority, we may then seek congruence between policy objectives and the political landscape upon which those objectives must rest. To begin to make these estimates, let us return to Lyon and Birmingham and specify the connections between political unity and policy control.

Political Structure and
the Course of Redevelopment

Birmingham's experience with Comprehensive Redevelopment does show how close government may come to unifying control over the redevelopment of an urban area. The Public Works Department closely approximated the planning ideal of one agent making all major decisions about investment within a specified area. At the same time this experience shows how fragile and elusive are the political requisites of this degree of control.

The Public Works Department maintained control over the Comprehensive Redevelopment Areas because others who might have compromised that control either could not or for their own reasons chose not to do so. The coincidence is considerable.

First of all, Parliament could at any time have directed any action it wished (save, according to Bagehot, to make a man a woman) within the Redevelopment Areas. As the law stood, however, agencies of the central government lacked the legal authority, the financial leverage, and the administrative wherewithal to intervene directly in shaping Birmingham's urban renewal strategy. While national planning and housing regulations and subsidies created a tight framework for redevelopment, no central agent exercised the control to effect changes within that frame.

Similarly, the legal structure of urban redevelopment, which was reinforced politically, provided little role for organizations or individuals outside government. Birmingham's access to Exchequer subsidies and to credit allowed the city to make investment decisions without shaping its plans or bending the program of implementation to the financial concerns of private investors.

More remarkable than the limited or indirect role of national government or private firms in Comprehensive Redevelopment was the Public Works Department's success in maintaining local political support. Unlike national government agencies and private firms, which had no legal role in the implementation of redevelopment, local political and administrative leaders might well have used the council's authority or other departments' administrative positions to insist on alterations in redevelopment plans. That these alterations did not occur is testimony first to the political skill of successive chief officers, but second to the solid political foundation local partisanship created.

Throughout the Comprehensive Redevelopment Program the local political parties effectively focused conflict away from the substance of urban renewal and allowed the planners a free hand in carrying out their projects. Most local elected officials were able to eschew returns to political entrepreneurship based on discontent with redevelopment. Their control of municipal politics hinged on the local two-party system, and the local two-party system in turn hinged upon mass and elite attachments to national party affiliations. To bring major, substantive local issues squarely onto Birmingham's political agenda would have threatened the stability of the political structure that served the established leaders of both major political parties. Liberals and other "community politics" types were occasionally to be tolerated but surely not to be imitated. As a result, no serious threat to professional domination of redevelopment emerged before the Labour Party's internal change and subsequent electoral success in the early 1970s.

The consequence of an urban renewal program dominated by planners and engineers was a coherently planned and implemented set of projects. Officials could translate their analysis of redevelopment needs into detailed strategies and apply those strategies in any area that fit a set of well-defined criteria. Insulation of the strategies' implementation from "outside" influence meant first that the plans could be fulfilled faithfully and second that they could be fulfilled in keeping with the current British housing policy, which called for maximum production of low-income municipal housing.

Comprehensive Redevelopment always had critics within the ministry and opponents within Birmingham's deteriorating neighborhoods.[4] Since, however, proredevelopment forces dominated both local parties and all important professional departments and since the two parties and the major departments controlled local political conflict, these critics and opponents had no access to the decisions affecting the course of the program. Changing concepts of urban renewal and dwindling support at the national level for massive clearance may gradually have slowed Birmingham's redevelopment bulldozer, but only a shift in the local political balance could have stopped it in its tracks.

The capture of Council House by a Labour group opposed to redevelopment led—as had always been possible—to the council's assertion of authority over the program and to an end to wholesale clearance. In so doing, the Labour group wrought not only a major change in the program's goals but, perhaps more important, a change in the way urban renewal would be carried out. The move from Comprehensive Redevelopment to neighborhood-based renewal meant that one organization would no longer dominate the planning and execution of renewal projects but that planning and, crucially, implementation would devolve to dozens of neighborhood groups, landlords, and home owners. The government would provide a fairly coherent set of incentives, but action would depend on literally dozens of separate decisions for each small sector of the city.

The increase in the complexity of implementation produced a considerable decline in the extent to which plans were fulfilled and in the scope of renewal activity. In part these changes were the conscious intent of Urban Renewal's advocates. The irony of the change, however, is that increased political access led directly to diminished production of improved inexpensive housing, housing that is, for precisely those whom the new Labour group most wished to aid.

Urban Renewal's advocates would surely have resisted an interpretation of their innovations as a choice between wholesale clearance and excruciatingly slow amelioration of low-income housing. In fact the change did not result from a clear position on this difficult policy dilemma but rather followed from an evolving political structure that motivated insurgent Labour politicians to adopt a community-based electoral strategy. Whatever the substantive impact of Urban Renewal may prove to be, the political time was surely ripe for those who advocated its principles.

Opponents of Birmingham's Comprehensive Redevelopment Program consciously reduced centralized control over urban renewal; advocates of redevelopment in Lyon struggled continuously to maintain the political, financial, and administrative support needed to achieve even minimal control over the implementation of renewal plans. Lyon's experience demonstrates the practical importance of control in fulfilling the purposes of urban renewal.

No agency in Lyon approached the Birmingham Public Works Department's domination of redevelopment. The partisan, administrative, and legal boundaries that protected Comprehensive Redevelopment, even Urban Renewal, and made such domination possible either never existed or were easily breached in Lyon. Instead successive individuals and groups acted as brokers among the various interests concerned with the planning and implementation of the projects. These brokers, of whom the mayor and the SERL were the most important, struggled to strike successive deals among groups that in Birmingham simply could not have demanded that their interests be built into the city's renewal program. From this difference grew the major contrasts between the two cities' programs.

This multiplicity of groups able to influence the course of urban renewal in Lyon resulted in the first instance from the program's legal base. French planning, regional development, and housing law distributed legal, technical, and financial resources among several central and local agencies. Agencies with different perspectives on redevelopment could, therefore, act to change ongoing projects or establish new projects of their own without much regard for an overall metropolitan strategy. If Birmingham provided a model of bureaucratic uniformity, insulation, and singularity of purpose, Lyon exemplified administrative complexity and overlap. Acting from Paris, from regional ministry field offices, or from various municipal departments, a comparatively large number of administrative agencies directly participated in the planning and execution of Lyon's renewal projects.

The investment strategies of Birmingham's property developers were essentially irrelevant to the implementation of urban renewal, but their counterparts were crucial in Lyon. Unless Lyon's projects could attract major private participation, they stood still. Thus another category of participant gained leverage over the content of the program.

Moreover, since private investment was much more responsive than public investment to short-term changes in real estate markets, the willingness of investors to participate in different kinds of projects changed over time. With changes in investor willingness came additional changes in the content of projects.

Perhaps a firm, durable political base for the municipal government could have focused the interests of these varied powers and interests into a consistent strategy and then forced participants to act as the plan dictated. Lyon's municipal leadership was surely durable, but the dominant coalition either could not or would not muster the political forces to insist upon those provisions of the plans that proved unpopular. Instead it supported projects that provided opportunities for a range of public and private firms and agencies, but resisted plans that disrupted the lives of many local citizens.

The result of this considerable dispersal of the wherewithal to shape urban renewal and the lack of the political strength to hold desperate actors together was Lyon's *coup par coup* redevelopment. The DDE's rather ambitious mid-1950s planning effort served to initiate debate, but the resulting document did not long serve to structure that debate, much less to structure the projects that followed. Lyon's projects were changeable, they covered a relatively small portion of the city, and they added less than they took from the low-income housing stock.

Political Structure and Synoptic Policymaking

The results of these case studies must be disconcerting for the policy analyst who sees "synoptic policymaking" and "coherent planning" as crucial to the success of government action in policies like urban renewal.[5] A government's means for making and implementing policy are complex and inconsistent, inconsistent not by accident or oversight but because the institutions of policymaking embody both diverse interests and the means to protect those interests. Both cities' experiences illustrate the process. As the agencies, firms, and individuals needed to see a plan through to its completion multiply, so the perspectives on that plan multiply. As perspectives increase, so do appraisals of costs and benefits, and so too demands for exceptions and alterations. In the end coherence gives way to patchwork, and those interests most crucial to the accomplishment of governments' aims have the greatest influence on the content of their actions.

Still a patchwork that pieces together the most important of interested parties could be the basis for a plan, perhaps even for a plan that is more responsive to diverse needs than an expert's product. Unfortunately for coherence, however, to agree to a plan is not necessarily to remain willing or able to act when one's own piece is needed. Comprehensive Redevelopment required nearly thirty years to complete two of its three portions; the Part-Dieu project needed almost twenty years to carry out a greatly reduced agenda. Over time, people, perspectives, and assessments change, and commitments weaken. More alterations and retrenchments occur as the "rigors of implementation"[6] press upon major participants.

Planning suffers because those who must act in concert to realize a plan are likely to care about other things more than they care about urban renewal or any other specific program. Elected officials care more about maintaining a coalition or a base of political support, investors care more about profits and losses, and bureaucrats care more about maintaining their agency's overall strength and responsibility. As a result, those who control the political, technical, and financial resources that major plans demand willingly use their positions to alter or limit plans in pursuit of these overarching ends.

These larger goals conflict, the positions of once like-minded participants diverge, and policymaking becomes a difficult task. Holistic planning of complex and important programs becomes a frustrated dream.

To say unlikely, is not to say never, and more important, it is not to say that plans will not, under the right political conditions, constrain urban redevelopment policy. We have in fact now returned to our original quest for the political conditions most conducive to the accomplishment of complex and intricate plans for the renewal of urban areas.

While changeable, these conditions are neither ephemeral or haphazard; they follow directly from the structural characteristics of political systems. They are part of what makes politics in one land different from politics in another. If, as we have seen, political structure creates in a given time and place organizations that shape public policy, patterns of compromise, conflict, and autonomy among those institutions determine what the content of these policies will be.

For the realization of complex, controversial programs like urban renewal, the most telling feature of a country's political structure is simply the number of these significant organizations the system actually produces— the extent of political fragmentation. The more that the authority and the resources to act or to block action were divided among both public and private organizations, the less likely were plans to be fulfilled. Greater fragmentation—whether the contrast is between Birmingham in two periods or between Birmingham and Lyon—meant that policymakers had to count on the cooperation of more actors with separate agendas and thus had to tolerate less predictable results; planning suffered proportionately.

"Number of participating organizations" will, however, serve poorly by itself as an indicator of political fragmentation. The willingness and ability of these organizations to dominate, persuade, or bribe their colleagues and rivals vary considerably. So does the probability that separate organizations will routinely cooperate. Consequently the intensity of fragmentation will also vary with the kind of organizations among which significant roles are divided. Involving an international real estate developer in the implementation of an urban redevelopment project or permitting a militant neighborhood association to veto plans for the same project are two ways in which fragmentation can be increased by one organization. The implications for planning will be rather different.

This formulation has two implications. First, as we have seen, countries with more institutional fragmentation will make public policy differently from those with less. Second, different countries and different cities within countries having similar levels of fragmentation may also differ significantly in their relative ability to realize tough policy objectives.[7] The experience of Lyon and Birmingham (as well as of other cities that have tried similar programs) with urban redevelopment now allows us to reach several conclusions, some rather surprising, about what levels of fragmentation, involving what sorts of organizations with what sorts of interrelationships are most important for the content of urban redevelopment policy.

The contrast between the British and the French urban planning apparatus provides us with a clear case in which the number of agencies contending for a role in policymaking is more important than the specific responsibilities any may hold. The effects of this contrast are also somewhat at odds with what might well be expected of the two countries. One might reasonably suppose that the well-articulated French administrative system would be relatively conducive to coherent urban policymaking. Rather than proliferating local planning fiefdoms, the Napoleonic state brings urban policy into one centralized hierarchy. Furthermore, the same system sends highly trained, well-connected civil servants to each urban center where they exercise a national mandate to pursue a coordinated urban program. Shouldn't such a clear centralizing presence ensure more adherence to plans than the British arm's length approach? Wouldn't the latter system leave planners more exposed to shifting political and economic fortunes than their French counterparts?

The case studies, of course, belie these suppositions. The presence of a putative centralizing institution does not by itself necessarily reduce political fragmentation; it may in fact increase it. A French political structure, which simultaneously gives considerable authority to organs of central government and considerable political leverage to agents of the cities, creates a political tension inimical to planning. More organizations, not fewer, act relatively independently at the operational level. Concentration of resources at this level, as in Britain, produces the opposite result.[8]

Though more centralized, the French urban planning apparatus is more fragmented than its British counterpart. The addition of national-level technical and financial organizations to the redevelopment process, whatever other good it may bring about, diffuses governmental authority and inhibits the realization of plans. Here the straightforward increase in number of actors is more important than the supposed national authority certain of them may embody. To decentralize territorially is not, in other words, necessarily to eviscerate governmental authority, although it has seemed to do so in the United States.

With other kinds of institutional divisions, however, the species of organization involved is of greater importance than the number; political parties are a case in point. A considerable, if inconsistently convincing, literature disputes the extent to which the ideological tendencies of the party in control of a municipal council determine the character of local policy.[9] The present study, in contrast, minimizes the importance of *party* as ideological or policy unity, but stresses *partisanship* as a component of fragmentation and a determinant of policy.

Elected officials in both Lyon and Birmingham surely pursued urban renewal policies that more or less fit their ideological commitments. Nevertheless, there is little evidence to suggest that local party doctrine had very much impact on the content of decisions made at the local level. The important contribution of local political parties was their relative ability to contain and focus local political conflict on their own terms, an ability that depended on partisanship.

Partisanship, the fealty of both citizens and their leaders to party organizations, acts as a potent antidote to political fragmentation. Where Tories remain loyal as municipal housing expands and Labourites dutifully accept the need to favor home owners at the expense of renters, political parties can protect redevelopment plans from those who see merit or gain in potential changes. Where a mayor's supporters begin to jump ship over the fate of a few buildings, plans are the perpetual hostage of coalition members and the factions they represent.

In neither Britain nor France are local political parties independent, autonomous organizations; they are parts of national networks. But since loyalty to the two major British parties extended to municipal issues, Birmingham's policymakers—both elected and professional—enjoyed a remarkable period of freedom from local factional conflict. Whatever attachment the major participants in Lyon's urban renewal program may have had to national parties, those party ties did not bind anyone's hands when specific redevelopment decisions were at stake. Again, Communists, Radicals, or Gaullists differed in their views of correct and just policy, but no party qua organization could demand adherence to a plan as a condition of party membership and effective participation in local politics. By dominating municipal elections and disciplining municipal councillors, the Birmingham Labour and Conservative parties capitalized upon partisanship and effectively exercised this kind of control. As a result, political fragmentation, while it increased over time, was lower in Birmingham than in Lyon.

In addition to fragmentation among territorial authorities and among local political factions, fragmentation also arose from the separation of planning from implementation.[10] This form of fragmentation appeared in two ways. In some instances, the government agencies authorized to develop renewal plans operated with political constituencies, professional doctrines, and financial constraints quite different from those of the agencies charged with implementing the plans. In other cases, implementation became the task of private firms and households quite outside the direct control of governmental officials. In either case, planning could fare well only if the needs and values of the implementers fit well with those of the planners; this situation rarely occurred.

The clearest illustration of the policy impact of this separation comes from Birmingham's shift from Comprehensive Redevelopment to Urban Renewal. As long as the Public Works Department could both design projects and undertake major portions of their accomplishment—acquisition, clearance, infrastructure construction—plans fit results. Faced with the Public Works Department's framework, other implementers—builders of schools, parks, or public housing—were in relatively weak positions to disrupt redevelopment plans.

Once the council took these powers to act away from the Public Works Department and its allies and limited the successor agency to drawing maps, planning no longer had the same meaning. No one's concept of a renewal area was likely to dominate when a myriad of households and loosely confederated neighborhood associations were responsible for the program's accomplishment. Under these conditions there was no reason to expect the planners' will to be done or to anticipate an insignificant number of bottlenecks and deviations.[11]

Throughout its program, Lyon provides a more typical example of the same effect. The private and public investors who put redevelopment plans into action simply did not accept the urbanization goals expressed in successive plans and used their discretion to reshape programs to fit their own needs and standards more closely. Again, small matter that some planning agencies were part of the national administration and others local. The Atelier d'Urbanisme and the planning sections of the DDE alike lacked the authority to imitate the Public Works Department's active pursuit of its own plans.

To the extent that the same people who compose plans have the opportunity to orchestrate and conduct them (or at minimum to carry out sufficient portions that other players are greatly constrained), projects should reflect a synoptic approach to policymaking. To the extent that these activities are divided and dispersed, projects will reflect a piecemeal and *coup par coup* character.

A special, important case of the separation between planning and implementation arises when projects require the financial participation of private investors to reach completion. Owing to what Lindblom calls the "privileged position of business," planners are under these circumstances especially weak. Lindblom argues in general terms that "businessmen generally and corporate executives in particular, take on a privileged role in government that is, it seems reasonable to say, unmatched by any leadership group other than government officials themselves."[12] Business leaders command the authority to invest, produce, and employ with the result that "governments in these market-oriented systems recognize that businessmen need to be encouraged to perform,"[13] and because "encourage" must mean induce rather than compel, "government leadership must often defer to business leadership. . . . Businessmen cannot be left knocking at the doors of the political systems, they must be invited in."[14] Inviting businessmen into urban redevelopment programs has consequences for both the process and the substance of resulting projects.

Whether operating in Detroit or Lyon, private investors will demand clear opportunities for profit in any project seeking their participation.[15] No one would expect them to act otherwise. But the attractiveness of different kinds of projects and any firm's ability to spend money will change over time and so will the willingness of investors to risk their funds. Consequently, the door to private participation must be open as public officials draw plans, and it must remain open as they attempt to implement them. Otherwise redevelopment planners may find themselves, as so often in the United States, with cleared land and no one to build.

This form of fragmentation, in which public agencies plan and private firms implement, is important because these organizations differ in their needs and purposes, not just because more actors are added. As Marx in the classic case saw Louis Napoleon squeezed between the demands of capital and the demands of the masses, so is conflict likely between the urban redevelopment goals of planners and those of private investors. Consequently, this division not only hampers the attainment of public control over urbanization; it modifies the ends that government can achieve.

To recognize this consequence is to solve the puzzle as to why urban renewal rarely produces low-cost, good quality housing even though legislation and initial plans often express a firm intent to do so. Unless that category of housing can generate as secure and attractive a return as available alternatives, investors will simply take their risks elsewhere. In fact they may even recognize that the site assembly and clearance aspects of urban renewal themselves make project areas especially attractive places for construction of high-cost housing or commercial buildings. Especially enterprising investors may even encourage public officials to provide urban renewal land for just such purposes. In this way public officials find themselves choosing among public investment, no investment, and private investment in buildings other than low-cost housing. Both policy control and social welfare content decrease. As Lindblom says, for important aspects of policymaking, "businessmen . . . must be invited in."

Consideration of the forms of political fragmentation most telling where urban policymaking is concerned, leads to two kinds of conclusions. First, the substance of what urban renewal projects accomplish will vary in ways that directly reflect ongoing political relations among the institutions important in the realization of the projects. Second, while urban renewal programs may bring about significant changes in some aspects of a city's form and character, only rarely will these programs in themselves greatly alter the ways cities change physically, socially, or economically. This latter conclusion follows jointly from the former and from the generally observable complexity of urban policymaking.

Synoptic Policymaking and the Revival of Cities

The dominant theme of this inquiry has been the differences in the results of public policy efforts that political contrasts cause. In particular I have been concerned with the tension between efforts to gain firm public control over public policy and the political fragmentation of governing institutions. We have seen that tension is important because policy initiatives like urban renewal take a concerted, unifying political arbiter for granted. They in fact assume political conditions rarely to be found. Fragmentation rather than concentration characterizes the institutions that typically make urban public policy.

Fragmentation, however, comes in a variety of sizes and shapes, each with specifiable consequences for the substance of public policy. Of particular importance are first the internal interests of the organizations among which responsibilities for policy realization are fragmented and second the presence of organizations able and willing to draw these organizations into concerted action. When a complex program involves a plurality of organizations with differing substantive objectives, the program will result in partial attainment of these objectives, compromises among these objectives, or, when settlements cannot be reached, stalemates.[16] In the common situation when crucial organizations are numerous and dependable cooperation does not follow from the organizations' own objectives, the probability of stalemates increases in a process that underscores the importance of a political arbiter, an organization that can "hold them all in awe." Where such organizations—Birmingham's two major political parties were examples—can use threats, side payments, and personal appeals to secure concerted action, considerable policy control can emerge out of potentially high levels of fragmentation. Where such organizations are weak or absent, policy control will also be weak.[17]

Consider the relationship between local political fragmentation and the results of urban renewal in a few prominent American cities, all operating under the same national program, administrative structure, and economic institutions. As long as a firm political-professional-business coalition endured, New Haven acted decisively and on a relatively large scale.[18] In Chicago, where a partisan organization dominated professional and business interests, urban renewal forged ahead but reversed its priorities to suit ward-based political leaders.[19] But in Toledo, with no political organization to take the initiative or the responsibility, urban renewal withered on the vine.[20] The realization of plans varied with the ability of planners to maintain a political base: the stability of that political base varied with the structurally defined fragmentation of political resources. Moreover, the content of realized programs reflected the interests and preferences of organizations that had to be satisfied if that political base was to endure.

The experiences of Lyon and Birmingham and of many cities in the United States in fact indicate that this political base probably will not survive the expense, controversy, and disruption of large-scale urban renewal. While the political conditions that facilitate the adoption and implementation of such difficult but important public programs can be named, their joint occurrence is exceptional. The presence in countless city archives of ambitious renewal plans vaguely represented in bricks and mortar is no accident, nor is it tribute to incompetence in urban policy analysis. This gap between plans and realization follows from the diffuse and polycentric environment in which urban policy is made.

For a variety of reasons, urban renewal could never have drastically altered urbanization patterns in industrialized countries and revived cities under severe economic and social pressure.

Comprehensive Redevelopment moved to Lyon or Chicago would not have stemmed the depopulation of the Massif Central or the Black Belt of America's Southeast any more than it could halt the decline of the British automobile industry. No urban program, however well planned and fully implemented, can reverse a nation's economic and demographic trends in a stroke. But for good political reasons even the more modest goals for physical change contained in urban renewal plans were rarely destined to be realized. Whatever the potential impact of fully implemented urban renewal, the nature of urban political conflict meant that full implementation was rarely a reasonable hope or a reliable basis for planning the course of public policy.

To summarize and generalize this conclusion: policymaking is invariably a political matter but not in a random or capricious manner. To agree that political structure conditions the content of public policy to a significant extent is to recognize a political system's limited propensity and capacity to pursue difficult courses of action. Public policy will roughly conform to the political landscape on which it is implemented. When, therefore, coherent plans do not match the existing political structure and the structure cannot be reshaped to match the plans, the ideal of synoptic policy will not be realized. Plans will either be rejected outright or reshaped to accommodate the political landscape.

This conclusion rests on the simple but often ignored fact that governmental action depends on the cooperation or at least the acquiescence of numerous organizations and individuals and that no important action will aid or penalize them all equally. As a result those groups and individuals who anticipate costs from a proposed action or greater benefits from an alternative will attempt to block action or secure changes. They will succeed in proportion to their ability to exercise power within the constraints of the political structure they face. Government action will, therefore, ultimately reflect the way in which political structure divides social power among political organizations. The prospects are probably slight that a political arbiter will rationalize this process in a way that suits planners.

This analysis implies that the advocate of governmental action (or inaction) that does not fit the existing political structure has two options, neither of which is to assume that other actors will discard political avenues useful in pursuing their own interests and preferences: either concentrate on designing policies that fit that landscape or bulldoze it into a shape that will support policies thought ideal in their own terms.

The durability of political structures does not rule out the latter alternative. Like a physical landscape, a political landscape does change in large and small ways. Important policy issues can become a cause as well as an effect of such change. The implementation of Comprehensive Redevelopment was a source as well as a result of the Public Works Department's influence over local policymaking. As the program grew, so did the budget, staff, and compass of the agency. Similarly, dissatisfaction with this massive program proved a rallying point for the department's opponents and one factor in its demise. The result was not only a change in the course of redevelopment but also a change in political structure that probably made the previous course impossible to resume.

This study revealed no other political change of this magnitude. The limited success in both cities of community organizations as the agents of neighborhood preservation indicates the difficulty of shaping political structure to fit policy objectives.

Nevertheless, when structural changes do occur and do involve significant redistributions of political resources, policy changes are likely to follow. Although Lyon and especially Birmingham experienced increases in political entropy during the period under consideration, other changes could involve the concentration rather than the fragmentation of political influence. The emergence of the SERL as the manager of *concertation* and its consequent gain in influence over redevelopment policy represented a move in this direction. A political system that consistently shows itself unable to deal effectively or justly with a range of significant policy issues might well induce change toward greater political concentration.

The policy advocate who judges structural change unpalatable or unlikely finds the range of action thereby constrained, even more constrained than many attempts at policy analysis would suggest. As Anton has written, "Recommendations that treat policy as mere technique, divorced from social relations that motivate and sustain it, often become proposals for fundamental system change, whether the authors realize it or not."[21] The attribution of important differences in policy outcomes to ongoing structural features of political systems implies, however, a conservative view of policy change. From this perspective, the design of programs must stress measures suitable for a political landscape that is on the whole given. The alternative is planning that merely speculates about how government action would be different if only politics wouldn't interfere.

Politics will always "interfere" because people will rarely accept unfavorable results when they have ready and sure means of opposition. As we have seen, this opposition is particularly telling when support does not mean acquiescence but active participation in a program's implementation. Those who have do not always get, but they can often avoid giving.

Effective planning, therefore, builds programs from an analysis of political constraints that is as careful as the analysis of economic, aesthetic, or geological forces. To call for a "bold and forceful program"[22] from a shaky, fragmented political base is to ignore analysis of this kind and invite the exact opposite of what was intended. Comprehensive, coherent policy follows from an equally comprehensive, coherent political base. Where such a base does not exist and cannot readily be built, policymakers must reduce their own aspirations to the attentive management of what will necessarily be a piecemeal and disorderly process.

Urban renewal in Lyon and Birmingham illustrates both success and failure in the pursuit of synopsis; it also illustrates attempts to manage the results of political fragmentation. Unlike Birmingham's Comprehensive Redevelopment Program, most urban policy initiatives must contend with a diffuse, polycentric political environment little conducive to the realization of complex controversial programs. We began in pursuit of the political conditions necessary to achieve synopsis in public policy; we conclude that urban policy should not be planned under the assumption that such conditions will exist.

On the one hand, this conclusion is regrettable. It implies that liberal governments are unlikely to realize truly major planned transformations of older urban areas. Political support is unlikely to develop fully enough or to be sustained long enough to allow for massive redevelopment on the scale of Birmingham's Comprehensive Redevelopment Program. When governments do undertake to revive older cities, they cannot expect the autonomy and political quiescence that Birmingham's planners enjoyed for over twenty-five years. Consequently, such efforts will be mixed in both the amount and the kinds of change they bring about. In this light it cannot be surprising that urban renewal quite accurately reflects prevailing distributions of social and economic power and the diverse objectives of the organizations that exercise that power.

Before, on the other hand, this inability is too much lamented, we need to take another comparative look at redevelopment in Lyon and Birmingham. For all the elegance of its planning and implementation, Birmingham emerged from its redevelopment programs as essentially the same nineteenth-century city with indoor plumbing, better ventilation, and sounder construction, changes that could not realistically be expected to stem the economic decline of such a city.[23] Lyon, however, for all its indecisiveness, did manage to obtain through redevelopment the superstructure of an important regional administrative and commercial center.

To say that Lyon's projects were executed in a piecemeal, unplanned fashion and that they occasioned considerable social change is also to say that these projects brought together a wide variety of perspectives on urban development and harnessed considerable amounts of private economic power. A large, modern city like Lyon or Birmingham focuses a wide variety of national, even international, economic and social processes. Is it reasonable or even wise to insulate major urban policies entirely from the impact of these processes? Have we given too much weight to synopsis and too little to a more accessible arena for those now left out of political conflict?

Notes

Chapter 1

1. For examples of central business district projects in New Haven and several English cities see Robert A. Dahl, *Who Governs? Democracy and Power in an American City*, pp. 113–140; and John Holliday, ed., *City Centre Redevelopment: A Study of British City Centre Planning and Case Studies of Five English City Centres*.

For examples of redevelopment that produced costly housing in Chicago, Boston, and Paris, see Peter Henry Rossi, *The Politics of Urban Renewal: The Chicago Findings*; Herbert J. Gans, *The Urban Villagers: Group and Class in the Life of Italian-Americans*; and Henri Coing, *Rénovation urbaine et changement social: l'îlot no. 4 (Paris 13ᵉ)*.

For examples of institutional redevelopment in Chicago and New York see Edward C. Banfield, *Political Influence: A New Theory of Urban Politics*, pp. 159–189; and Robert A. Caro, *The Power Broker: Robert Moses and the Fall of New York*, pp. 1013–1014.

For an example of substantial low-income housing production in Liverpool, see David M. Muchnick, *Urban Renewal in Liverpool: A Study of the Politics of Redevelopment*, esp. pp. 28–31.

For examples of a public works and economic development orientation in Atlanta, see Stanley B. Greenberg, *Politics and Poverty: Modernization and Response in Five Poor Neighborhoods*, pp. 32, 36; and Clarence N. Stone, *Economic Growth and Neighborhood Discontent: System Bias in the Urban Renewal Program of Atlanta*.

For an example of effective planning in Newcastle, see Jon G. Davies, *The Evangelical Bureaucrat: A Study of a Planning Exercise in Newcastle-upon-Tyne*.

For examples of aborted projects in Newark and Toledo, see Harold Kaplan, *Urban Renewal Politics: Slum Clearance in Newark*; and Jean L. Stinchcomb, *Reform and Reaction: City Politics in Toledo*, pp. 129–150.

2. For surveys of various national programs see "Urban Renewal" under country headings in Arnold Whittick, ed., *Encyclopedia of Urban Planning*.

3. Daniel P. Moynihan, "Policy vs. Program in the 1970s," in *Coping: On the Practice of Government*, p. 273.

4. Charles E. Lindblom, *Politics and Markets: The World's Political-Economic Systems*, p. 319.

5. I. M. Destler, *Presidents, Bureaucrats, and Foreign Policy: The Politics of Organizational Reform*, p. 1.

6. United States, President's Urban and Regional Policy Group, *A New Partnership to Conserve America's Communities: A National Urban Policy*, p. 6.

7. James H. Bater, *The Soviet City: Ideal and Reality*, p. 47.

8. David Gordon has argued that the suburbanization of industry can better be explained as an attempt to increase labor discipline. With major instances of suburban worker unrest—the Pullman strike in 1894 and the Battle of the Bridge at Ford's River Rouge Plant in 1937—immediately preceding the two major waves of suburbanization, however, managers cannot easily have associated suburban isolation with docility. The search for social and economic segregation probably explains more of residential than industrial suburbanization. I would not entirely exclude political motivation from explanations of either. See David Gordon, "Capitalist Development and the History of American Cities," in William K. Tabb and Larry Sawers, eds., *Marxism and the Metropolis: New Perspectives in Urban Political Economy*, pp. 25–63. On residential suburbanization see Michael N. Danielson, *The Politics of Exclusion*, pp. 1–26.

9. Dahl, *Who Governs?*, p. 201.

10. For a full development of this case of the "Prisoners' Dilemma," see Jerome Rothenberg, *Economic Evaluation of Urban Renewal: Conceptual Foundations of Benefit-Cost Analysis*, p. 40.

11. Ibid., p. 47.

12. For a summary of U.S. legal provisions see Ashley A. Foard and Hilbert Fefferman, "Federal Urban Renewal Legislation," in James Q. Wilson, ed., *Urban Renewal: The Record and the Controversy*, pp. 93–94, 96–97. For France see France, Ministère de la Réconstruction et du logement, *La lutte contre le taudis et la rénovation de l'habitat défecteux*, pp. 21–24; André Poissonier, *La rénovation urbaine*; and Richard L. Ludwig, "Administrative Systems for Urban De-

velopment and Renewal: The Case of Urban Renewal in France." For Great Britain; see Great Britain, Ministry of Town and Country Planning, *Town and Country Planning Act, 1944: Explanatory Memorandum*; and John English, Ruth Madigan, and Peter Norman, *Slum Clearance: The Local and Administrative Context in England and Wales*.

13. In France and increasingly in Britain and the United States an influential group of neo-Marxist scholars tells a similar story from a different perspective. Urban redevelopment from this view is the attempt of the monopoly sector of capital to wrench control of cities from workers and the traditional middle classes. Evidence for this interpretation is the repeated adoption of redevelopment strategies best suited to further social segregation within metropolitan areas, even when such strategies neglect housing, economic growth, and land-use patterns, the announced goals of the programs. This interpretation explains one powerful interest's strategy for redevelopment; it does not explain what will happen when that or any other interest attempts to realize its goals in a given city at a given time. As these scholars have themselves documented, resistance to social segregation can have a significant impact on the content of redevelopment programs. The discussion that follows asks whether any strategy for urban redevelopment, whether it serves the interests of monopoly capital, municipal bureaucrats, or low-income residents, can be coherently realized. This approach should identify a single dominant interest if and when it occurs and specify the political conditions under which it emerges. The neo-Marxist explanation of corporate capital's interest in urban redevelopment is quite compatible with my analysis. I, however, will concentrate on how interests are translated into brick and concrete rather than on how interests are generated. For both, the state's attempt to gain control over urban change is a central political question. For discussions of urban redevelopment in France, see Francis Godard, Manuel Castells, et al., *La rénovation urbaine à Paris: structure urbaine et logique de classe*; Manuel Castells, "Urban Renewal and Social Conflict in Paris"; Jean Lojkine, *La politique urbaine dans la région lyonnaise, 1945–1972*, pp. 139–144. For a similar interpretation in the United States, see John H. Mollenkopf, "The Postwar Politics of Urban Development," and Chester Hartman and Rob Kessler, "The Illusion and Reality of Urban Renewal: San Francisco's Yerba Buena Center," in Tabb and Sawers, eds., *Marxism and the Metropolis,*

pp. 117–178. For the issues of control treated from a Marxist perspective, see Jean Lojkine, "L'état et l'urbain: contribution à une analyse materialiste des politiques urbaines dans les pays capitalistes développés," esp. pp. 264–265.

14. Hugh Heclo, *Modern Social Policies in Britain and Sweden: From Relief to Income Maintenance*, p. 9.

15. Alan P. Altshuler, *The City Planning Process: A Political Analysis*, pp. 314–315.

16. Ibid., p. 311.

17. This formulation is somewhat anthropomorphic. The argument is, in fact, that the logic of organizational maintenance and the extent of organizational resources both constrain and motivate the behavior of organizational leaders in predictable ways. The result looks approximately like organizational behavior. The argument is spelled out in James Q. Wilson, *Political Organizations*, esp. Chs. 3 and 5.

18. These translate literally as: Public Facilities and Housing Ministry, Organization for Development Studies for the Lyon Metropolitan Area, Central Corporation for Territorial Public Facilities. These and all subsequent translations are mine.

19. The population of the City of Lyon in 1975 was 457,410 and that of Birmingham in 1979 was 1,033,900. The population of Marseille proper is larger than that of the commune of Lyon, but the latter is the center of a more populous metropolitan area.

20. In 1968, 45.6 percent and in 1975, 45.0 percent; France, Institut national de la Statistique et des études économiques, *Recensement de la population*, 1968 and 1975.

21. West Midlands Economic Planning Council, *The West Midlands Patterns of Growth*, p. 10.

22. France, Organisation d'Etude d'aménagement de l'aire métropolitaine Lyon-Saint-Etienne-Grenoble, *Schéma d'aménagement de la métropole Lyon-Saint-Etienne-Grenoble: métropoles d'équilibre et aires métropolitaines*, p. 72. Great Britain, Department of Economic Affairs, *The West Midlands: A Regional Study*, p. 41.

23. Tertius Chandler and Gerald Fox, *3000 Years of Urban Growth*, p. 133.

24. B. R. Mitchell, *European Historical Statistics, 1750–1970*, p. 76.

25. Chandler and Fox, *3000 Years*, p. 157.

26. Mitchell, *European Historical Statistics*, p. 77. This figure in-

cludes several annexed industrial suburbs, but given the concentration of growth in these areas, the figures are not misleading.

27. West Midland Group on Post-War Reconstruction and Planning, *Conurbation: A Planning Survey of Birmingham and the Black Country*, pp. 15–16; and Neville Borg, "Notes Given to Councillor Price, Chairman, Public Works Committee, 29/7/54," p. 1.

28. André Bruston, "La 'régénération' de Lyon: une intervention dans la transformation du tissu urbain" (paper presented at Ministère de l'Equipement colloquium, "Politiques urbaines et planification des villes," Dieppe, August 8–10, 1974), p. 5.

29. Jacques Bonnet, *Les villes françaises: Lyon et son agglomeration*, p. 9. Bruston quotes 5,900 for 1800; "La 'régénération' de Lyon," p. 5.

30. Bonnet, *Les villes françaises*, p. 13.

31. West Midland Group, *Conurbation*, pp. 91, 89.

32. Borg, "Notes," p. 1.

33. For details on original construction see Conrad Gill, *History of Birmingham*, vol. 1, pp. 367–369.

34. Pierre de Boissieu, "Centres de propagande et d'action contres les taudis: la réstauration immobilière à Lyon", p. 8. In Lyon, as in much of France, housing construction was at a virtual standstill between the two world wars.

35. City of Birmingham, *Report of the Medical Officer of Health for the Year 1945*, p. 76; and City of Birmingham, *Report of the Medical Officer of Health for the Year 1946*, p. 93.

36. Interview, *Post* (Birmingham), November 9, 1953.

37. Herbert J. Manzoni, "Duddeston and Nechelles Redevelopment Areas," p. 8.

38. Neville Borg, "Redevelopment in Practice."

39. City of Birmingham, Housing Department, "The Balance between Conservation and Improvement," p. 3.

40. Ibid., p. 1.

41. City of Birmingham, *Abstract of Statistics*, no. 1, p. 67; no. 14, p. 112.

42. City of Birmingham, Public Works Department, "Memorandum on Housing in Birmingham during the Post-War Period."

43. Ted Taylor, "Urban Renewal—The Corporate Approach."

44. Reg Bowen, "The Concept and Management of Urban Renewal."

45. Brian Shuttleworth, "Urban Renewal in Birmingham."

46. Mr. J. A. Charman of the City of Birmingham Environmental Health Department kindly provided these statistics in a private communication. For a similar view see Chris Paris, "Birmingham: A Study in Urban Renewal."

47. France, Ministère de la Construction, Direction départementale du Rhône, "Plan directeur d'urbanisme de la région lyonnaise: mémoire explicatif général."

48. It also listed Saint-Jean, Lyon's historical preservation sector.

49. France, Ministère de la Construction, "Plan directeur d'urbanisme," p. 38.

50. Ibid., p. 48.

51. J. Dubois and F. Loizy, "Rapport sur la rénovation des îlots urbains défecteux des quartiers des Brotteaux et du Tonkion à Lyon," pp. 4–5.

52. Alain Mechain, "Réhabilitation, restauration, rénovation, restructuration: une certaine politique urbaine: analyse critique de 6 opérations," p. 144.

53. Interview, *Le Progrès de Lyon*, April 15, 1957. The other project was a sports arena.

54. Unless otherwise noted descriptions of successive plans for the Part-Dieu are derived from models and plans shown me at the Atelier d'Urbanisme de Lyon, the Société d'Equipement de la région lyonnaise, or the Direction départmentale d'Equipement.

55. *Echo-Liberté*, February 27, 1960.

56. *Vie lyonnaise*, March 1962.

57. Bonnet, *Les villes françaises*, p. 56.

58. M. Rollet, "Bulletin municipal official de Lyon," p. 147.

59. De Boissieu, "Centres de propagande," pp. 6 ff. Additional descriptive material is derived from interviews with Association de Restauration immobilière officials and neighborhood association members.

60. Rent control is still imposed on French housing built before 1948. Rents in Place Forez increased from 100 to 120 francs a month to 250 or 300 francs a month.

61. Mechain, "Réhabilitation," p. 9.

62. France, Ministère de la Construction, "Plan directeur d'urbanisme," p. 48.

63. Charles Delfante, "Urbanisme: La Part-Dieu dans Lyon," p. 7.

64. Neville Borg, "Birmingham," in Holliday, ed., *City Centre Redevelopment*.

Chapter 2

1. Ivo Duchacek, *Comparative Federalism: The Territorial Dimension of Politics*, p. 4.

2. See ibid. for a list of examples.

3. I concentrate here upon delegation to territorial authorities and largely overlook the implications of delegation according to function. For a careful treatment of relationships between these two forms of delegation, see James W. Fesler, *Area and Administration*.

4. For a further discussion of the theoretical issues behind this argument, see Douglas E. Ashford, "Territorial Politics and Equality: Decentralization in the Modern State," esp. pp. 71–75.

5. E. E. Schattschneider, *The Semisovereign People: A Realist's View of Democracy in America*, p. 11. James Fesler makes a similar argument in "Approaches to Understanding Decentralization," p. 551.

6. Schattschneider, *The Semisovereign People*, p. 40.

7. For example, see Theodore J. Lowi, *The End of Liberalism: Ideology, Policy, and the Crisis of Public Authority*, esp. pp. 85, 271–274.

8. Grant McConnell, *Private Power and American Democracy*, esp. pp. 166–168.

9. Sidney G. Tarrow, *Between Center and Periphery: Grassroots Politicians in Italy and France*, p. 27.

10. For examples of comparisons between France and Great Britain, see Frank Smallwood, *Greater London: The Politics of Metropolitan Reform*, pp. 138–139; F. F. Ridley and Jean Blondel, *Public Administration in France*, p. 85; and Brian Chapman, *Introduction to French Local Government*, p. 22.

11. The *départements* date as administrative units from the French Revolution. They were set up in an attempt to quell provincial dissension by dividing the old provinces into quite small territorial units susceptible to rule by a delegate from Paris. There are currently ninety-five *départements*. For a discussion of the history of French field administration and its role in the development of the modern, unified state, see James W. Fesler, "French Field Administration: The Beginnings"; Fesler, "The Political Role of Field Administration"; and Ezra N. Suleiman, *Politics, Power, and Bureaucracy in France: The Administrative Elite*, pp. 14–16.

12. Howard Machin, "The French Prefects and Local Administration," p. 237. For a less skeptical statement, see Chapman, *Introduction to French Local Government*, p. 22.

13. Maurice Bourjol, *Droit administrative 1.: l'action administrative*, p. 104.

14. Ridley and Blondel, *Public Administration in France*, pp. 104–105.

15. Mark Kesselman, *The Ambiguous Consensus: A Study of Local Government in France*; Laurence Wylie, *Village in the Vaucluse*. We might see American cities in a similar light if we looked at similar places. Compare Arthur J. Vidich and Joseph Bensman, *Small Town in Mass Society: Class, Power, and Religion in a Rural Community*. Also see Machin, "The French Prefects," p. 248.

16. Cabinet ministers must resign from the Chamber of Deputies but not from city hall.

17. Jean-Claude Thoenig, "La relation entre le centre et la périphérie," p. 87.

18. Tarrow, *Between Center and Periphery*, p. 147.

19. Jack Hayward and Vincent Wright, "The 37,708 Microcosms of an Indivisible Republic: The French Local Elections of 1971," p. 290.

20. Pierre Grémion and Jean-Pierre Worms, "L'état et les collectivités locales," p. 26.

21. Tarrow, *Between Center and Periphery*, pp. 153–154.

22. Ridley and Blondel, *Public Administration in France*, p. 112; Suleiman, *Politics, Power, and Bureaucracy*, pp. 239–281.

23. Suleiman, *Politics, Power, and Bureaucracy*, pp. 279–281.

24. Control over the Directions départementales was a major issue in the protracted warfare between the Ministère de la Construction et du logement and the Ministère des Travaux publics and between the elite Corps des Ponts et chaussées and the not quite so elite Corps des Travaux publics. See Suleiman, *Politics, Power, and Bureaucracy*, pp. 274–275 and J.-C. Thoenig, *L'ère des technocrates: le cas des Ponts et chaussées*.

25. France, Ministère de la Construction, "Plan directeur d'urbanisme"; and Dubois and Loizy, "Rapport sur la rénovation," pp. 4–5.

26. Mayors in other cities also recognized that they could only have an important role in local land-use planning if they controlled sufficient expertise and had sufficient points of intervention. Joint local-central planning became, for this reason, an important feature of the *Loi d'ori-*

entation foncière (Land Guidelines Act) of 1967. See François d'Arcy and Bruno Jobert, "Urban Planning in France," in Jack Hayward and Michael Watson, *Planning, Politics and Public Policy: The British, French and Italian Experience*, p. 301.

27. See Thoenig, "La relation entre le centre et la périphérie," p. 86; and Tarrow, *Between Center and Periphery*, p. 58 for a similar argument.

28. For example an official from the Direction départementale d'Equipement du Rhône was in 1975 appointed associate director of the Atelier d'Urbanisme of Lyon. In Birmingham, officials in ministry field offices could think of a few cases in which officials from local administration had taken positions with the central administration; the reverse was unknown.

29. For a history of this important institution, see Roger Priouret, *La Caisse des Dépôts: cent cinquante ans d'histoire financière.*

30. D'Arcy and Jobert, "Urban Planning in France," p. 297.

31. S E Ms also build and manage a variety of other public facilities, such as parking garages, subway systems, and toll roads.

32. François d'Arcy, *Structures administratives et urbanisation: la S C E T*, p. 81.

33. Ibid., p. 42.

34. Mark Kesselman, "Overinstitutionalization and Political Constraint: The Case of France," p. 37; Suzanne Berger, et al., "The Problem of Reform in France: The Political Ideas of Local Elites," pp. 449–450; and Tarrow, *Between Center and Periphery*, pp. 57–58.

35. Thoenig, "La relation," pp. 105–106. S C E T and S E R L officials in particular emphasized their ability to deal with metropolitan area mayors of all political parties.

36. France, Ministère de la Construction, "Plan directeur d'urbanisme," p. 48.

37. On February 29, 1960, the Conseil municipal actually delegated responsibility for the project to the S E R L. Discussions of purchase terms and plans for the sector had occupied the three or four preceding years. For a chronology, see *Vie lyonnaise*, March 1962.

38. For a brief summary of these programs see James L. Sundquist, *Dispersing Population: What America Can Learn from Europe*, pp. 91–145. For additional detail see Niles M. Hansen, *French Regional Planning.*

39. This phrase originates in the now classic J. F. Gravier, *Paris et*

le désert français. Characteristically, the *Economist* aptly summarized the basic political principle: "If the right in France holds the countryside and the left holds the towns, what happens when everybody lives in Paris?," January 25, 1975, p. 23.

40. Others were Lille-Roubaix-Tourcoing, Nancy-Metz, Strasbourg, Marseille-Aix-Berre, Toulouse, Bordeaux, and Nantes-Saint-Nazaire.

41. Jérôme Monod, *Transformation d'un pays: pour une géographie de la liberté*, p. 43.

42. Tarrow, *Between Center and Periphery*, pp. 57–58.

43. Monod, *Transformation d'un pays*, p. 48.

44. *Dernière Heure de Lyon*, July 17, 1965.

45. *Le Progrès de Lyon*, October 28, 1967, and August 3, 1969.

46. Coing, *Rénovation urbaine et changement social.*

47. De Boissieu, "Centres de propagande"; Great Britain, Ministry of Housing and Local Government and the Welsh Office, "Old Houses into New Homes"; Great Britain, Secretary of State for the Environment and Secretary of State for Wales, "Widening the Choice: The Next Steps in Housing."

48. De Boissieu, "Centres de propagande," p. 5.

49. The phrase, of course, comes from Morton Grodzins, *The American System: A New View of Government in the United States.*

50. Ridley and Blondel, *Public Administration in France*, p. 56.

51. L. J. Sharpe, "Modernizing the Localities: Local Government in Britain and Some Comparisons with France," in Jacques Lagroye and Vincent Wright, eds., *Local Government in Britain and France: Problems and Prospects*, p. 44.

52. Ibid.

53. The Department of the Environment was created in 1970 from the Ministry of Housing and Local Government, the Ministry of Transport, and the Ministry of Public Buildings and Works. Of course other departments, e.g., the Home Office (police and fire) and the Ministry of Education and Science, have specific dealings in particular subject areas.

54. Evelyn Sharp, *The Ministry of Housing and Local Government*, p. 214.

55. Ibid., p. 20.

56. Ibid., p. 24.

57. The effects of heading a "headquarters department" can be seen in activities reported by former Minister of Housing Richard Cross-

man. Much of Crossman's day was spent adjudicating interauthority conflicts, hearing final planning appeals, and fighting political fires related to ministry concerns. When he routinely visited local authorities, his tours and briefings were handled by representatives of the local government. Crossman's *The Diaries of a Cabinet Minister*, vol. 1, pp. 400–401, contains a good illustration that is relevant to Birmingham's development program.

58. A quantity surveyor, an important professional figure in the British building industry, draws up from architects' plans specifications for required building materials and estimates their costs.

59. J. A. G. Griffith, *Central Departments and Local Authorities.*

60. Griffith, *Central Departments*, p. 276.

61. Ibid., p. 260; S. E. M. Sadek, *The Balance Point between Local Autonomy and National Control*, p. 38. For an indication of the detail and specificity of regulations, see the so-called Parker-Morris standards for municipal housing in Great Britain, Ministry of Housing and Local Government, *Homes for Today and Tomorrow.*

62. These considerations are, however, important. See Howard A. Scarrow, "Policy Pressures by British Local Government: The Case of 'Regulation in the Public Interest,'" p. 11; and Noel Boaden, "Central Departments and Local Authorities: The Relationship Examined," p. 177.

63. Great Britain, Department of the Environment and the Welsh Office, "Fair Deal for Housing," p. 14.

64. Douglas E. Ashford, "Are Britain and France 'Unitary'?," p. 489.

65. The procedures followed also showed marked differences. Similarly, Douglas E. Ashford has shown that the increases over time of central aid to municipal budgets were not correlated with the amount of variation in expenditures among various local authorities; see "The Effects of Central Finance on the British Local Government System." Considerable variation has also been found by Noel Boaden, *Urban Policy-Making: Influences on County Boroughs in England and Wales*; and J. Alt, "Some Social and Political Correlates of County Borough Expenditures."

66. James W. Fesler, "Approaches to the Understanding of Decentralization," p. 554.

67. Ibid. For a careful historical analysis of the triumph of "nationalized" politics over "localism" and thus the subordination of local

to national electoral goals, see Ken Young, *Local Politics and the Rise of Party: The London Municipal Society and the Conservative Intervention in Local Elections*.

68. Austin Ranney, *Pathways to Parliament: Candidate Selection in Britain*, pp. 280–281.

69. Paul E. Peterson, "British Interest Group Theory Reexamined: The Politics of Comprehensive Education in Three English Cities," p. 388; G. W. Jones, *Borough Politics: A Study of the Wolverhampton Town Council, 1888–1964*, p. 324.

70. The sale of council houses was a contentious partisan issue, but it was largely symbolic, a "gnat bite," one civil servant commented. Only a few hundred of Birmingham's council houses were sold between 1966 and 1972, out of a total of over 100,000.

71. For the history of the dispute, see Peterson, "British Interest Group Theory," p. 386.

72. Jones, *Borough Politics*, p. 326.

73. Both the Conservative and the Labour parties can, but rarely do, veto constituency organization candidate choices; see Ranney, *Pathways*, pp. 42–51, and 161–164.

74. John Gyford, *Local Politics in Britain*, p. 19.

75. Ibid.

76. A Birmingham Conservative leader claimed that local politicians listened to the central office in direct proportion to their desire for honours. I asked a Conservative Central Office official about Birmingham Conservative leader Sir Francis Griffin's flouting Tory principles by supporting large amounts of municipally rented housing. "I guess," he replied, "people around here just assume that a man like Sir Francis knows what he's doing." Note that Griffin received his knighthood anyway.

77. Lowi, *The End of Liberalism*, p. 212.

78. Ashford, "Are France and Britain 'Unitary'?," p. 494.

79. I should emphasize, however, that the same party simultaneously controlled Birmingham Council House and Westminister for only two extended periods during the years considered in this study: October 1964 through March 1966 and February 1974 through May 1976. The major topic then at issue between Birmingham and London—the use of Greenbelt land for municipal housing—was resolved no more favorably for Birmingham during that period than after the Tory takeover in Birmingham in 1966.

80. Stanley Hoffman, *Decline or Renewal? France since the 1930s*, p. 454.

81. Sharpe, "Modernizing British Local Government," in Lagroye and Wright, eds., *Local Government in Britain and France*, p. 46.

82. Elements of the following material are drawn from transcripts of conversations held between Manzoni and Dr. Anthony Sutcliffe of the Economic History Department of the University of Sheffield. I am grateful to Dr. Sutcliffe for his generous assistance.

83. Birmingham was the only city to take advantage of this act's provisions before the 1947 act limited their application.

84. For a detailed legislative history see David H. McKay and Andrew W. Cox, *The Politics of Urban Change*, pp. 116–144.

85. Great Britain, Department of the Environment, "Slums and Older Housing: An Overall Strategy," p. 16.

86. One exception to this pattern is the Grande Côte project, which the city undertook on its own.

Chapter 3

1. Wallace S. Sayre and Herbert Kaufman, *Governing New York City: Politics in the Metropolis*, p. 712.

2. Banfield, *Political Influence*, p. 235.

3. Douglas T. Yates, *The Ungovernable City*, p. 5.

4. Dahl, *Who Governs?*, p. 235.

5. Altshuler, *The City Planning Process*, pp. 310–311.

6. For a detailed description of Moses's career see Caro, *The Power Broker*.

7. Banfield, *Political Influence*, p. 237.

8. Peter B. Clark and James Q. Wilson, "Incentive Systems: A Theory of Organizations."

9. For a review of attempts to deal with this question, see Robert C. Fried, "Comparative Urban Performance," in Fred I. Greenstein and Nelson W. Polsby, eds., *The Handbook of Political Science*, vol. 6.

10. For contrasts between public housing programs in Chicago and New York see Martin Meyerson and Edward C. Banfield, *Politics, Planning, and the Public Interest: The Case of Public Housing in Chicago*, pp. 294–298; for contrasts among War on Poverty programs in five cities see David Greenstone and Paul E. Peterson, *Race and Authority in Urban Politics: Community Participation and the War on Poverty*, esp. pp. 19–43.

11. David Butler and Donald Stokes, *Political Change in Britain: Forces Shaping Electoral Choice,* pp. 469, 488, 502.

12. Ibid., p. 43.

13. Ibid., p. 13.

14. For descriptions of nominating procedures see W. Hampton, *Democracy and Community: A Study of Politics in Sheffield,* pp. 62–63; and Jones, *Borough Politics,* pp. 97–99.

15. All county boroughs (the largest municipal authorities before reorganization) reported in a Ministry of Housing and Local Government study that they operated on a "party basis"; Great Britain, Committee on the Management of Local Government, *Management of Local Government,* vol. 5: *Local Government Administration in England and Wales,* p. 97. Details of partisan control and its methods may be found in any of the numerous case studies of individual municipalities. See for examples, Hampton, *Democracy and Community,* on Sheffield; Jones, *Borough Politics,* on Wolverhampton; H. W. Wiseman, "The Working of Local Government in Leeds," on Leeds; and J. G. Bulpitt, *Party Politics in English Local Government,* on four Lancashire cities.

16. Note that the key group is the Council Party Group, councillors belonging to a common political party. Each of these groups acted like "a law unto itself" for council matters, largely unrestrained by the local party organizations. See Ken Newton, *Second City Politics: Democratic Processes and Decision-Making in Birmingham,* pp. 100–101, 103.

17. The only major breach of discipline in recent memory occurred in 1963 when several Labour Party councillors voted against a Labour Group-sponsored resolution to raise rents paid by municipal housing tenants. Although the increase passed the council, the rebels were asked for formal apologies and excluded from the Labour Group when they refused. Having found insufficient support for their positions within the group, or in ward party organizations, the councillors submitted the apologies and were reinstated. See Newton, *Second City Politics,* pp. 259–262.

18. This procedure, in fact, required an act of Parliament. Local property taxes could not be set nor could money be borrowed without vote of the full council.

19. On occasions when the balance of seats in the council was extremely close, some minor chairmanships were assigned to minority party members.

20. L. James Sharpe, "In Defence of Local Politics," in Sharpe, *Voting in Cities: The 1964 Borough Elections*, p. 13.

21. For similar observations on the operation and importance of specialized committees in British cities, see Jones, *Borough Politics*, p. 177; Scarrow, "Policy Pressures by British Local Government," p. 17; and L. James Sharpe, "American Democracy Reconsidered: Part I," pp. 21–22.

22. Labour controlled the council from 1945 until 1948, from 1952 until 1966, from 1972 until 1976, and after 1979; Conservatives were in the majority in other years.

23. This last issue, a major one throughout Britain in the 1960s, involved Conservative advocacy of and Labour opposition to examination requirements for entrance into elite secondary schools (grammar schools). The Labour Party proposed that all students be sent to comprehensive schools.

24. Thomas J. Anton, *Governing Greater Stockholm: A Study of Policy Development and System Change*, p. 142.

25. Ibid., p. 161.

26. Sayre and Kaufman, *Governing New York City*, p. 406.

27. But ministers also find themselves dominated by highly able technical advisers. See Crossman, *The Diaries of a Cabinet Minister*; or Hugh Heclo and Aaron Wildavsky, *The Private Government of Public Money: Community and Policy in British Political Administration.*

28. Scarrow observes the same tendency in "Policy Pressures by British Local Government," p. 19.

29. Before the 1974 reorganization, the town clerk was the city's legal counsel, election supervisor, and policy coordinator.

30. He cited an incident in which a Labour Party leader had assembled a group of chief officers and private building contractors and had browbeaten them into advancing and rearranging construction timetables to permit an early start on a highly visible municipal housing project.

31. Municipal election results are from *The Birmingham Post Year Book and Who's Who*; S. R. Aymer, "Pressure Groups and Local Education Administration," p. 12; and the *Times* of London.

32. In fact the Liberal Party reemerged throughout England between 1966 and 1974. Whether Liberal successes in Birmingham reflected this national development or some purely local political force is of no consequence for present purposes. We need only be concerned with the local politicians' *assumption* that local factors were crucial.

For an example of the importance attributed to Liberal successes in Birmingham's inner wards, see long-time municipal reporter John Falding's prediction that the Liberals might emerge in the 1970s as the major opposition party to the Birmingham Tories, *Birmingham Post*, May 20, 1969.

33. Liberal leader Wallace Lawler, who died in 1972, made these remarks in an interview with Dr. Anthony Sutcliffe on December 11, 1967. I am grateful to Dr. Sutcliffe for providing me with a transcript of this conversation.

34. The most influential work describing this phenomenon is Michael Young and Peter Willmott, *Family and Kinship in East London*. Written specifically about the effects of redevelopment in Birmingham are Norman S. Power, *The Forgotten People: A Challenge to a Caring Community*; and Thomas L. Blair, *The Poverty of Planning*. American works from this mold are exemplified by Gans, *The Urban Villagers*; and Gerald D. Suttles, *The Social Order of the Slum*.

35. Shuttleworth had been among those particularly active in developing a personal constituency in his ward. See *Birmingham Mail*, April 29, 1969.

36. This view received official endorsement in the Skeffington report; Great Britain, Ministry of Housing and Local Government, the Scottish Development Department, and the Welsh Office, Committee on Public Participation in Planning, *People in Planning*. A public health inspector, who had processed condemnation orders for Redevelopment Areas, commented, "These young arrogant politicians—your age—they hear some sociologist talking about breaking up communities. I've broken up more communities than anyone else, and I'm proud of it."

37. I do not mean to impute any measure of cynicism to these men and women. When discussing urban renewal, each stressed a humanitarian rather than an electoral motivation for the reassessment of the program and of the neighborhood. I have stressed the electoral and organizational politics of the situation because I think it is no accident that a group of politicians with this particular view of humanitarian policy gained prominence at this particular time.

38. In fact interpenetration was probably greater for urban renewal than for other local policy issues.

39. Philip E. Converse and Georges Dupeux, "Politicization of the Electorate in France and the United States," in Angus Campbell, et

al., *Elections and Political Order*, p. 277. The following pages of this article discuss the relationship between this low level of mass partisanship and general characteristics of the French party system. Their argument is updated and applied to political socialization in Greg A. Caldeira and Fred I. Greenstein, "Partisan Orientation and Political Socialization in Britain, France, and the United States." An Institut français pour l'opinion publique survey conducted in January 1967 (cited in Sidney Tarrow, "The Urban-Rural Cleavage in Political Involvement: The Case of France," p. 347) found a party identification among only 32.6 percent of respondents. In cities like Lyon, with populations of more than 100,000 located outside the Paris region, the comparable figure was 34.2 percent.

40. The important exception, of course, is the Communist Party whose adherents formed the most dependable French voting bloc.

41. Philip Williams, "Party, Presidency, and Parish Pump in France," pp. 257–258. Tarrow argues that both local and national politicians had reasons to inhibit this translation; *Between Center and Periphery*, pp. 57–58.

42. Kesselman, "Overinstitutionalization," pp. 35–36; and Elisabeth Dupoirier and Gérard Grundberg, "Vote municipal et vote legislatif. Evolution de 1965 à 1971 dans villes de 30,000 habitants." The unusual municipal election system in force for the 1965, 1971, and 1977 elections was, in fact, designed to encourage electoral polarization. Voters chose among complete lists of candidates for the municipal council. All members of the list that received an absolute majority in the first election or a plurality in the second took all council seats and elected the head of their list mayor. There were in most cities no opposition council members; the council was composed entirely of "running mates." In Lyon, Marseille, and Paris lists were elected by sector or ward creating the possibility of opposition members. Pradel's electoral success was great enough that his list won all nine sectors in 1965 and 1972. The union of the left won two sectors and twelve seats in 1977.

43. Jerome E. Milch, "Paris Is Not France: Policy Outputs and Political Values in Two French Cities," vol. 2, p. 525, dicusses a local Socialist who completed a "political odyssey from Socialist to Communist to Gaullist in less than a decade." Also see Mark Kesselman, "Political Parties and Local Government," p. 24.

44. Even national politicians like Jacques Chelban-Delmas and

Gaston Defferre seem to establish a local following for municipal purposes quite distinct from support derived from their roles in national
politics. See Henry Ehrmann, *Politics in France*, pp. 90–91. Compare
L. J. Sharpe's discussion of the difficulties faced by a British municipal
politician who wishes to achieve a similar distinction in "American Democracy Reconsidered: Part II," p. 135.

45. Colette Ysmal, "L'élection de M. Gaston Defferre à Marseille,"
p. 344; and Jerome E. Milch, "Influence as Power: French Local Government Reconsidered."

46. Williams, "Party, Presidency, and Parish Pump," p. 260.

47. Grémion and Worms, "L'état et les collectivités locales," p. 31.
Tarrow argues that one important reason for the failure of national political parties to penetrate to the level of municipal politics is the concern of municipal officials that partisanship will interfere with patterns
of administrative complicity. Sidney Tarrow, *Partisanship and Political
Exchange in French and Italian Local Politics: A Contribution to the
Typology of Party Systems*, p. 43.

48. The 1971 muncipal election in Toulouse provides an illuminating contrast. The Socialist incumbent, who lacked the support and cooperation of the central administration, was defeated by a Gaullist
challenger with government support. The new mayor, remarkably, had
served as subprefect in Toulouse before contesting the election.

49. Dahl, *Who Governs?*, pp. 309–310.

50. Like other large cities, Lyon had no independent muncipal administration during the Vichy regime. Herriot spent that period in
internment.

51. Allocation of seats in the 1947 and 1953 Lyon municipal elections:

List	1947	1953
Parti radical	16	15
Indépendant	—	16
Parti communiste français	13	13
Rassemblement du peuple français	23	7
Mouvement républicain populaire	6	4
Section français de l'Internationale ouvrière	—	3

Source: *Le Progrès de Lyon*, April 29, 1953.

52. For example, Herriot submitted his resignation to the prefect in 1955 when the council elected a Radical member to replace a deceased Indépendant assistant mayor. The Radical promptly resigned allowing the right man to be elected and Herriot to return. *Le Progrès de Lyon*, March 15, 1955.

53. For a chronology of the making and breaking of coalitions, see *Le Progrès de Lyon*, April 15, 1957.

54. Pradel publicly expressed his astonishment at his election and maintained that he had not been a candidate; ibid. Privately, Pradel boasted self-deprecatingly that he had been selected because he was "la plus con" (which may very euphemistically be translated as the "biggest turkey") of all the council members.

55. Hayward and Wright, "The 37,708 Microcosms," p. 301. Lojkine argues that Pradel's grip was possible because of the concentration of artisans and small enterprises in Lyon. The relative absence of large firms inhibited class politics; Lojkine, *La politique urbaine*, pp. 17–18.

56. For the commercial, trade union, and professional affiliations of Pradel's 1959 list, see *Le Progrès de Lyon*, February 27, 1959.

57. Or, as the *Canard Enchâiné* would have it, "Pour la Recuperation Abusive des Electeurs Leurrés."

58. Percent of vote in municipal elections, by list, 1965, 1971, and 1977:

List	1965	1971	1977 1st round	1977 2nd round
PRADEL	69.54	66.39	43.20	54.20
Union pour la nouvelle république	10.01	—		
Parti communiste français–Parti socialiste unifié	18.37	6.71		
Union de Gauche	—	28.06	33.10	45.70
Rassemblement pour Lyon (Soustelle)	—		7.40	
Lyon-Ecologie			8.70	
GUIGNOL			3.30	
Extreme left			3.00	
Moderate majority			1.20	

No second round was held in 1965 or 1971 because the PRADEL list captured an absolute majority of votes in the first round. Totals may not equal 100 percent because of rounding error.

59. An exception was made for the hero of the Free French and villain of Algeria, Jacques Soustelle. Soustelle led the UNR list against Pradel in 1965. In 1971 Pradel accepted Soustelle on his list and faced no opposition from the national majority coalition. See Hayward and Wright, "The 37,708 Microcosms," p. 301, for a slightly different interpretation.

60. In 1968 Lyon and fifty-six neighboring communes were by act of the Assembly joined into the Communauté urbaine de Lyon—the Courly. Thereafter, all major urban planning and development issues were in principle under the jurisdiction of the Courly rather than the constituent communes, which retained authority for smaller public works and school construction. I gloss over this distinction for two reasons. First, of the projects under consideration here, only the latter phases of the Part-Dieu and Martinière-Tolozan actually came under the Courly's jurisdiction. All others remained with the City of Lyon, which either had initiated the projects or still retained sufficient powers for their accomplishment. Second, the Courly council was elected by the constitutent communal councils according to each commune's proportion of the metropolitan population. Because Lyon contained just over half the Courly's residents, a majority of Courly council members were members of the PRADEL list from the City of Lyon, and Pradel served as the Courly's president. Thus the Courly operated according to political principles congruent with the city's. Among those principles was the maximum retention of autonomy by the constituent communes. Pradel insisted that Courly employees refer to him as "M. le maire" rather than "M. le president" and continued to use his city hall Lyon office. On Lyon's domination of the Courly, see Lojkine, *La politique urbaine*, p. 27.

61. The Atelier's staff and director became Courly employees in 1968.

62. In his study of Nîmes and Montpellier, Milch also notes a congruence between the local council coalition and the delegation of administrative responsibility; "Paris Is Not France," vol. 1, pp. 181, 185, 188, 192.

63. For early plans see *Le Progrès de Lyon*, September 25, 1956, February 24, 1958, June 5, 1958; and *Vie lyonnaise*, March 1962.

64. Tarrow makes a similar argument but connects it to centraliza-tion. He contends that building broad coalitions "may be the French mayor's strategic response to his lack of effective policy choice and an admission that he could not *implement* the kind of programs that an ideologically more coherent local coalition might force him to sup-port"; *Betwen Center and Periphery*, p. 246.

65. Sylvie Biarrez, et al., *La place de l'institution communal dans l'organisation de la domination politique de classe en milieu urbain: le cas de Roanne*, p. 94.

Chapter 4

1. Andrew Shonfield, *Modern Capitalism: The Changing Balance of Public and Private Power*, p. 99.

2. Ibid., p. 128.

3. Ibid., p. 94.

4. Ibid., p. 156.

5. Jack Hayward, "Politics of Planning in France and Britain—Trans-Atlantic View," p. 287; and Hayward, "Choice and Change: The Agenda of Planning," in Hayward and Watson, eds., *Planning, Politics and Public Policy*, p. 14.

6. François Bloch-Lainé, *A la recherche d'une "économie concer-tée*," p. 6.

7. Samuel H. Beer, *British Politics in a Collectivist Age*, p. 329. Contrast this view with the reluctance of French bureaucrats to say anything favorable about interest groups. See Suleiman, *Politics, Power, and Bureaucracy in France*, pp. 325–326.

8. Shonfield, *Modern Capitalism*, p. 160.

9. For a detailed example in another policy area, see Harry Eck-stein, *Pressure Group Politics*.

10. Hayward, "Politics of Planning," pp. 287–288.

11. "Tutor" poorly translates the role ministries play in *la tutelle*. The term originates in administrative law and designates the domi-nation of a superior over an inferior but quasi-independent agency. "Ward" and "guardian" may be more accurate translations. See Chap-ter 2.

12. Hayward, "Choice and Change," in Hayward and Watson, eds., *Planning, Politics and Public Policy*, pp. 7–8. Suleiman, *Politics, Power, and Bureaucracy*, p. 347.

13. Suleiman, *Politics, Power, and Bureaucracy*, p. 330.

14. Ibid., pp. 330–346.

15. Shonfield makes this argument in several places; see *Modern Capitalism*, pp. 128 ff. See also Suleiman, *Politics, Power, and Bureaucracy*, pp. 337–346; and Suleiman, "Industrial Policy Formulation in France," in Steven J. Warnecke and Ezra N. Suleiman, eds., *Industrial Policies in Western Europe*.

16. There is some evidence that these relationships may be quite different for Britain. See Hayward, "Politics of Planning," p. 296; and Paul E. Peterson and Paul Kantor, "Citizen Participation, Political Parties, and Democratic Theory: An Analysis of Local Politics in England."

17. Tarrow argues that this bias extends to allocation choices among cities but does not himself extend the argument to firms or sectors within cities; *Between Center and Periphery*, pp. 76, 96.

18. Joseph LaPalombara, *Interest Groups in Italian Politics*, pp. 284–285.

19. Ibid.

20. While in control of the council, the Labour Group did make sure that the city conducted its labor relations in ways acceptable to the Trades Council. Again, however, I would not consider this important concession to have had systematic effects on redevelopment.

21. Hayward draws this contrast between the relative strength of economic planners and urban planning executives; "Politics of Planning," p. 296.

22. For examples, see Greenstone and Peterson, *Race and Authority in Urban Politics*; and Douglas T. Yates, *Neighborhood Democracy: The Politics and Impacts of Decentralization*.

23. The urban renewal officer was an official of the Housing Department and did not enjoy the independent staffing authority of departmental chief officers.

24. LaPalombara, *Interest Groups*, p. 322.

25. Ibid., p. 331.

26. Ibid., p. 333.

27. Ibid., p. 343.

28. Ibid., p. 316.

29. France, Ministère de l'Equipement et du logement, "Document de juin 1970," quoted in Paul Boury, "Les zones d'aménagement: urbanisme réglementaire et opérationnel," p. 22. My italics.

30. France, Commission des villes pour le VIᵉ plan, "Titre II," quoted in A.-H. Mesnard, *La planification urbaine*, p. 36.

31. Ibid.

32. Ibid., pp. 35–36. A Ministère de l'Equipement circular also stresses planning based on specified zones for joint public-private action. See Boury, "Les zones d'aménagement," p. 24.

33. Paul Boury, *La rénovation urbaine dans l'aménagement de territoire: ses origines, ses objectifs, sa technique, ses résultats, ses perspectives*, p. 2.

34. For an example of the same hitch in an American city's urban renewal program, see Harold Kaplan, *The Politics of Urban Renewal*, pp. 15–16. For a more general treatment, the search for the "blight that's right," see Charles Abrams, *The City Is the Frontier*, pp. 115–116.

35. George Captier, "Social Aspects of Urban Renewal in France," in International Union of Local Authorities, *Renewal of Village and Town*, p. 30.

36. Jean Lojkine documents the city's minimal budgetary commitment to low-income housing in *La politique urbaine*; see esp. pp. 67–71.

37. It is important to remember that in 1970 the central government was attempting to promote Lyon as a *"métropole d'équilibre"* and was especially anxious to support efforts to develop Lyon's tertiary sector. Here is another example of direct but limited central intervention in local policy development.

38. The project's director estimated that rents of 100 to 120 francs per month would increase to 250 to 300 francs, but by agreement with ARIM they could not be raised again for six years. A local journalist estimated even lower increases. *Vie lyonnaise*, November 12, 1970, p. 22.

39. The agency was organized by directors of the local low-income housing corporations, the local Order of Architects, and several land developers ("liberal developers," the ARIM director assured me).

40. The ARIM director complained at length about landlords' preference for entrusting rehabilitation work to the management firms that had been their buildings' "family doctors." Use of these firms, he claimed, made any attempt at grouped restoration impossible.

41. Lyon is not unusual in this respect. A Gaullist politician observed: "France suffers from lack of a major urban redevelopment policy. Outside of projects on empty spaces (belonging chiefly to the army as at Renne or Montpellier) or restoration of certain historic quarters

(la Marais), most projects are dragging"; Paul Granet, *Changer la ville*, pp. 80–81.

42. Only in the Grande Côte did a city agency, the Parks Department, buy, clear, and redevelop (as a public park) an urban renewal site.

43. Boury, *La rénovation urbaine*, p. 113.

44. France, Organisation d'Etude d'aménagement de l'aire métropolitaine Lyon-Saint-Etienne-Grenoble; Région Rhône-Alps, *Schéma d'aménagement*, p. 126.

45. Lojkine, *La politique urbaine*, p. 107.

46. Ibid., p. 192.

47. Manuel Castells, *The Urban Question: A Marxist Approach*, p. 322.

48. Ibid., p. 316.

49. Ibid., pp. 316–319.

50. Manuel Castells, "Urban Renewal and Social Conflict in Paris," p. 105. For a complete report of the Paris urban renewal study, see Godard, Castells, et al., *La rénovation urbaine*.

51. Lojkine, *La politique urbaine*, p. 77.

52. A similar theoretical approach is broadened to allow for municipal politics in Biarrez, et al., *La place de l'institution communale*.

53. LaPalombara, *Interest Groups*, p. 262.

Chapter 5

1. Bernard J. Frieden and Marshall Kaplan, *The Politics of Neglect: Urban Aid from Model Cities to Revenue Sharing*, p. 237.

2. Neville Borg, "Redevelopment in Practice," pp. 8–9.

3. The argument is spelled out fully in Otto A. Davis and Andrew B. Whinston, "The Economics of Urban Renewal," in Wilson, ed., *Urban Renewal*, pp. 50–67.

4. For a fairly early example in Birmingham, see Power, *The Forgotten People*.

5. Lindblom argues that experts are particularly likely to "misperceive their role" and pursue synopsis at the expense of effective advocacy of their own positions; *Politics and Markets*, pp. 323–324.

6. Jeffrey L. Pressman and Aaron Wildavsky, *Implementation*.

7. At a given time and place, the course of policy processes will also vary with the issue at question.

8. In principle, the same result should follow from a similar con-

centration at the national level. Difficulties, however, arise from this strategy in large, diverse nations. For a prominent example of national-level urban planning and its difficulties, see William Taubman, *Governing Soviet Cities*.

9. For examples, see Terry N. Clark, ed., *Comparative Community Politics*.

10. This issue is treated in Pressman and Wildavsky, *Implementation*; and in Eugene Bardach, *The Implementation Game: What Happens after a Bill Becomes a Law*, esp. pp. 43–46. I am indebted to Donald A. Kates for illuminating discussions of the impact of this separation on community health care planning.

11. For better or worse, community participation is not, therefore, a boon to comprehensive urban planning.

12. Lindblom, *Politics and Markets*, p. 172.

13. Ibid., p. 173.

14. Ibid., p. 175.

15. For an account of urban renewal's susceptibility to the vagaries of private development, see Roger Montgomery, "Improving the Design Process in Urban Renewal," in Wilson ed., *Urban Renewal*, pp. 454–487.

16. Of course, programs may totally neglect the objectives of other organizations or individuals whose political position did not assign them access to resources crucial to the realization of the program.

17. Unless, of course, the political system is so little fragmented that one organization firmly controls policymaking.

18. Dahl, *Who Governs?*, pp. 115–140, 185–220; and Raymond E. Wolfinger, *The Politics of Progress*, pp. 267–356.

19. Meyerson and Banfield, *Politics, Planning, and the Public Interest*.

20. Stinchcombe, *Reform and Reaction*, Chs. 3–6, 10, 11.

21. Anton, *Governing Metropolitan Stockholm*, p. 166.

22. President Jimmy Carter used this phrase hopefully at a moment of considerable disarray in his energy policy. Its equivalent has, however, been used by a variety of activists and analysts in almost every policy area. Richard Halloran, "President to Outline Energy Plan on TV," *New York Times*, July 3, 1979, p. D12.

23. Some have, in fact, argued a direct connection between Comprehensive Redevelopment and economic decline in Birmingham. See the *Financial Times*, July 18, 1978, "Birmingham," p. 15.

Bibliography

Among the principal sources for chronicling the succession of urban renewal plans and political events were the excellent newspaper clippings files in the Lyon city archives and at the Birmingham Post and Mail offices. I have cited articles from the *Birmingham Post*, the *Birmingham Mail*, *Le Progrès de Lyon*, *La Dernière heure*, *La Vie lyonnaise*, and *Echo-Liberté*. In addition I have quoted material from the *Times* (London), the *Financial Times* (London), the *Economist*, and the *New York Times*.

Abrams, Charles. *The City Is the Frontier*. New York: Harper Colophon, 1965.

Almond, Gabriel and Coleman, James S., eds. *The Politics of Developing Areas*. Princeton: Princeton University Press, 1961.

Alt, J. "Some Social and Political Correlates of County Borough Expenditures." *British Journal of Political Science* 1 (January 1971): 49–62.

Altshuler, Alan P. *The City Planning Process: A Political Analysis*. Ithaca: Cornell University Press, 1965.

Anton, Thomas J. *Governing Greater Stockholm: A Study of Policy Development and System Change*. Berkeley: University of California Press, 1975.

Ashford, Douglas E. "Are Britain and France 'Unitary'?" *Comparative Politics* 9 (July 1977): 483–499.

———. "The Effects of Central Finance on the British Local Government System." *British Journal of Political Science* 4 (July 1974): 305–322.

———. "Territorial Politics and Equality: Decentralization in the Modern State." *Political Studies* 27 (March 1979): 71–83.

Aymer, S. R. "Pressure Groups and Local Education Administration." M.Soc.Sci. thesis. University of Birmingham, 1971.

Banfield, Edward C. *Political Influence: A New Theory of Urban Politics*. New York: Free Press, 1961.

Bardach, Eugene. *The Implementation Game: What Happens after a Bill Becomes a Law*. Cambridge: MIT Press, 1977.

Bater, James H. *The Soviet City: Ideal and Reality*. Beverly Hills, Calif.: Sage Publications, 1980.

Beer, Samuel H. *British Politics in a Collectivist Age*. Rev. ed. New York: Vintage Press, 1969.

Berger, Suzanne; Gourevitch, Peter; Higonnet, Patrice; and Kaiser, K. "The Problem of Reform in France: The Political Ideas of Local Elites." *Political Science Quarterly* 84 (September 1969): 436–459.

Biarrez, S.; Bouchet, C.; Du Boisberranger, G.; Mingasson, C.; Monzies, M.; Pouyet, C.; with Kukawa, P. *La place de l'institution communal dans l'organisation de la domination politique de classe en milieu urbain: le cas de Roanne*. Grenoble: Centre de recherche de l'institut d'études politiques de Grenoble, 1972.

Birmingham, City of. *Abstract of Statistics*. Birmingham: City of Birmingham Central Statistical Office, 1977.

Birmingham, City of, Health Department. *Report of the Medical Officer of Health*. Birmingham: City of Birmingham Health Department, 1945, 1946, 1965.

Birmingham, City of, Housing Department. "The Balance between Conservation and Improvement." Birmingham: Housing Department Occasional Paper, 1973.

Birmingham, City of, Public Works Department. "Memorandum on Housing in Birmingham during the Post-War Period." Mimeographed. Birmingham, August 1944.

The Birmingham Post Year Book and Who's Who. Birmingham: The Birmingham Post & Mail, 1945–1978.

Blair, Thomas L. *The Poverty of Planning*. London: MacDonald, 1973.

Bloch-Lainé, François. *A la recherche d'une "économie concertée."* Paris: Les Editions de l'épargne, 1974.

Boaden, Noel. "Central Departments and Local Authorities: The Relationship Examined." *Political Studies* 18 (June 1970): 175–186.

———. *Urban Policy-Making: Influences on County Boroughs in England and Wales*. Cambridge: The University Press, 1971.

Bonnet, Jacques. *Les villes françaises: Lyon et son agglomeration*. Paris: La Documentation Française, 1975.

Borg, Neville. "Notes Given to Councillor Price, Chairman, Public
    Works Committee, 29/7/54." Vol. 1, no. 13, Borg Papers.
———. "Redevelopment in Practice." Lecture to Town Planning In-
    stitute. Birmingham, November 20, 1953. Vol. 2, pp. 8–9, Borg
    Papers.
Bourjol, Maurice. *Droit administrative 1.: l'action administrative.*
    Paris: Masson et Cie., 1972.
Boury, Paul. *La rénovation urbaine dans l'aménagement de territoire:
    ses origines, ses objectifs, sa technique, ses résultats, ses perspec-
    tives.* Paris: Europrint, 1970.
———. "Les zones d'aménagement: urbanisme réglementaire et opé-
    rationnel." *Moniteur des Travaux publics et du batiment.* April
    1973.
Bowen, Reg. "The Concept and Management of Urban Renewal." Pa-
    per presented to the Urban Renewal Seminar, Birmingham City
    Council, September 23, 1974.
Bruston, André. "La 'régénération' de Lyon: une intervention dans la
    transformation du tissu urbain." Paper presented at Ministère de
    l'Equipement colloquium, "Politiques urbaines et planification des
    villes," Dieppe, August 8–10, 1974.
Bulpitt, J. G. *Party Politics in English Local Government.* New York:
    Barnes and Noble, 1967.
Butler, David and Stokes, Donald. *Political Change in Britain: Forces
    Shaping Electoral Choice.* New York: St. Martin's Press, 1969.
Caldeira, Greg A. and Greenstein, Fred I. "Partisan Orientation and
    Political Socialization in Britain, France, and the United States."
    Political Science Quarterly 93 (Spring 1978): 35–49.
Campbell, Angus; Converse, Philip E.; Miller, Warren E.; and Stokes,
    Donald E. *Elections and the Political Order.* New York: John Wiley
    and Sons, 1966.
Caro, Robert A. *The Power Broker: Robert Moses and the Fall of New
    York.* New York: Alfred A. Knopf, 1974.
Castells, Manuel. *The Urban Question: A Marxist Approach.* Trans-
    lated by Alan Sheridan. London: Edward Arnold, 1977.
———. "Urban Renewal and Social Conflict in Paris." *Social Science
    Information* 11 (April 1977): 93–124.
Chandler, Tertius and Fox, Gerald. *3000 Years of Urban Growth.* New
    York: Academic Press, 1974.

Chapman, Brian. *Introduction to French Local Government*. London: George Allen and Unwin, 1953.

Clark, Peter B. and Wilson, James Q. "Incentive Systems: A Theory of Organization." *Administrative Science Quarterly* 6 (September 1961): 219–266.

Clark, Terry N., ed. *Comparative Community Politics*. New York: Halstead Press, 1974.

Coing, Henri. *Rénovation urbaine et changement social: l'îlot no. 4 (Paris 13ᵉ)*. Paris: Les Editions Ouvrière, 1966.

Crossman, Richard. *The Diaries of a Cabinet Minister*. London: Hamish Hamilton and Jonathan Cape, 1975.

Dahl, Robert A. *Who Governs? Democracy and Power in an American City*. New Haven: Yale University Press, 1961.

Danielson, Michael N. *The Politics of Exclusion*. New York: Columbia University Press, 1976.

d'Arcy, François. *Structures administratives et urbanisation: la S C E T*. Paris: Berger-Levrault, 1968.

Davies, Jon G. *The Evangelical Bureaucrat: A Study of a Planning Exercise in Newcastle-upon-Tyne*. London: Tavistock Publication, 1972.

De Boissieu, Pierre. "Centres de propagande et d'action contres les taudis: la restauration immobilière à Lyon." Internship thesis, Ecole nationale d'administration, 1967.

Delfante, Charles. "Urbanisme: La Part-Dieu dans Lyon." Report to the Société de l'Equipement de la région lyonnaise. Mimeographed. Lyon, 1969.

Destler, I. M. *Presidents, Bureaucrats, and Foreign Policy: The Politics of Organizational Reform*. Princeton: Princeton University Press, 1974.

Dubois, J. and Loizy, F. "Rapport sur la rénovation des îlots urbains défecteux des quartiers des Brotteaux et du Tonkin à Lyon." Report to the Ministère de la Reconstruction et du logement. Direction départmentale du Rhône, 1957.

Duchacek, Ivo. *Comparative Federalism: The Territorial Dimension of Politics*. New York: Holt, Rinehart and Winston, 1970.

Dupoirier, Elisabeth and Grundberg, Gérard. "Vote municipal et vote legislatif. Evolution de 1965 à 1971 dans villes de 30,000 habitants." *Revue française de science politique* 22 (April 1972): 238–269.

Eckstein, Harry. *Pressure Group Politics.* Stanford: Stanford University Press, 1960.

Ehrmann, Henry. *Politics in France.* Boston: Little, Brown and Company, 1968.

English, John; Madigan, Ruth; and Norman, Peter. *Slum Clearance: The Local and Administrative Context in England and Wales.* London: Croom Helm, 1976.

Fesler, James W. "Approaches to the Understanding of Decentralization." *Journal of Politics* 27 (August 1965): 536–567.

———. *Area and Administration.* University: University of Alabama Press, 1949.

———. "French Field Administration: The Beginnings." *Comparative Studies in Society and History* 5 (October 1962): 76–111.

———. "The Political Role of Field Administration." In *Papers in Comparative Public Administration,* ed. Ferrel Heady and Sybil L. Stokes, pp. 117–143. Ann Arbor: Institute of Public Administration, University of Michigan, 1962.

France, Institut national de la statistique et des études économiques. *Recensement de la population.* Paris: INSEE, 1968 and 1975.

France, Ministère de la Construction, Direction départementale du Rhône. "Plan directeur d'urbanisme de la région lyonnaise: mémoire explicatif général." Mimeographed. Lyon, 1961.

France, Ministère de la Reconstruction et du logement. *La lutte contre le taudis et la rénovation de l'habitat défecteux.* Paris: Imprimerie national, n.d. (circa 1959).

France, Organisation d'Etude d'aménagement de l'aire métropolitaine Lyon-Saint-Etienne-Grenoble; Région Rhône-Alps. *Schéma d'aménagement de la métropole Lyon-Saint-Etienne-Grenoble: métropoles d'équilibres et aires métropolitaines.* Paris: La Documentation française, 1971.

Frieden, Bernard J. and Kaplan, Marshall. *The Politics of Neglect: Urban Aid from Model Cities to Revenue Sharing.* Cambridge: MIT Press, 1977.

Gans, Herbert J. *The Urban Villagers: Group and Class in the Life of Italian-Americans.* New York: Free Press, 1962.

Gill, Conrad. *History of Birmingham.* Vol. 1. London: Oxford University Press, 1952.

Godard, Francis; Castells, Manuel; et al. *La rénovation urbaine à*

Paris: structure urbaine et logique de classe. Paris: Mouton, 1973.

Granet, Paul. *Changer la ville.* Paris: Bernard Grosset, 1975.

Gravier, J. F. *Paris et le désert français.* Paris: Flammerion, 1958.

Great Britain, Committee on the Management of Local Goverment, *Management of Local Government.* Vol. 5: *Local Government Administration in England and Wales.* London: H M S O, 1967.

Great Britain, Department of Economic Affairs. *The West Midlands: A Regional Study.* London: H M S O, 1965.

Great Britain, Department of the Environment. "Slums and Older Housing: An Overall Strategy." Circular 50/72. London: H M S O, 1972.

Great Britain, Department of the Environment and the Welsh Office. "Fair Deal for Housing." Cmnd. 4728. London: H M S O, 1971.

Great Britain, Ministry of Housing and Local Government. *Homes for Today and Tomorrow.* Report of a Sub-committee of the Central Housing Advisory Committee, Sir Parker-Morris, chairman. London: H M S O, 1961.

Great Britain, Ministry of Housing and Local Government and the Welsh Office. "Old Houses into New Homes." Cmnd. 3602. London: H M S O, 1968.

Great Britain, Ministry of Housing and Local Government, the Scottish Development Department, and the Welsh Office, Committee on Public Participation in Planning. *People in Planning.* London: H M S O, 1969.

Great Britain, Ministry of Town and Country Planning. *Town and Country Planning Act, 1944: Explanatory Memorandum.* London: H M S O, 1946.

Great Britain, Secretary of State for the Environment and Secretary of State for Wales. "Widening the Choice: The Next Steps in Housing." Cmnd. 5280. London: H M S O, 1973.

Greenberg, Stanley B. *Politics and Poverty: Modernization and Response in Five Poor Neighborhoods.* New York: John Wiley and Sons, 1974.

Greenstein, Fred I. and Polsby, Nelson W., eds. *Handbook of Political Science,* vol. 6. Reading, Mass.: Addison-Wesley, 1975.

Greenstone, J. David and Peterson, Paul E. *Race and Authority in Urban Politics: Community Participation and the War on Poverty.* New York: Russell Sage Foundation, 1973.

Grémion, Pierre and Worms, Jean-Pierre. "L'état et les collectivités locales." *Esprit* 38 (January 1970): 20–35.

Griffith, J. A. G. *Central Departments and Local Authorities*. London: George Allen and Unwin, 1966.

Grodzins, Morton. *The American System: A New View of Government in the United States*. Chicago: Rand McNally, 1966.

Gyford, John. *Local Politics in Britain*. London: Croom Helm, 1976.

Hampton, W. *Democracy and Community: A Study of Politics in Sheffield*. London: Oxford University Press, 1970.

Hansen, Niles M. *French Regional Planning*. Bloomington: Indiana University Press, 1968.

Hayward, Jack. "Politics of Planning in France and Britain—Trans-Atlantic View." *Comparative Politics* 7 (January 1975): 285–298.

Hayward, Jack and Watson, Michael, eds. *Planning, Politics and Public Policy: The British, French and Italian Experience*. London: Cambridge University Press, 1975.

Hayward, Jack and Wright, Vincent. "The 37,708 Microcosms of an Indivisible Republic: The French Local Elections of 1971." *Parliamentary Affairs* 24 (Autumn 1971): 284–311.

Heady, Ferrel and Stokes, Sybil L., eds. *Papers in Comparative Public Administration*. Ann Arbor: Institute of Public Administration, University of Michigan, 1962.

Heclo, Hugh. *Modern Social Politics in Britain and Sweden: From Relief to Income Maintenance*. New Haven: Yale University Press, 1974.

Heclo, Hugh and Wildavsky, Aaron. *The Private Government of Public Money: Community and Policy in British Political Administration*. Berkeley: University of California Press, 1974.

Hoffman, Stanley. *Decline or Renewal? France since the 1930s*. New York: Viking Press, 1974.

Holliday, John, ed. *City Centre Redevelopment: A Study of British City Centre Planning and Case Studies of Five English City Centres*. London: Charles Knight and Co., 1973.

International Union of Local Authorities. *Renewal of Village and Town*, vol. 5, no. 2. The Hague: Martinus Nijhoff, 1965.

Jones, G. W. *Borough Politics: A Study of the Wolverhampton Town Council, 1888–1964*. London: Oxford University Press, 1969.

Kaplan, Harold. *The Politics of Urban Renewal*. New York: Columbia University Press, 1963.

——. *Urban Renewal Politics: Slum Clearance in Newark*. New York: Columbia University Press, 1963.

Kesselman, Mark. *The Ambiguous Consensus: A Study of Local Government in France*. New York: Alfred A. Knopf, 1967.

——. "Overinstitutionalization and Political Constraint: The Case of France." *Comparative Politics* 3 (October 1970): 21–44.

——. "Political Parties and Local Government." Paper presented to the 1972 annual meetings of the American Political Science Association, Washington, D.C., September 1972.

Lagroye, Jacques and Wright, Vincent, eds. *Local Government in Britain and France: Problems and Prospects*. London: George Allen and Unwin, 1979.

LaPalombara, Joseph. *Interest Groups in Italian Politics*. Princeton: Princeton University Press, 1964.

Lindblom, Charles E. *Politics and Markets: The World's Political-Economic Systems*. New York: Basic Books, 1977.

Lojkine, Jean. "L'état et l'urbain: contribution à une analyse materialiste des politiques urbaines dans les pays capitalistes développés." *International Journal of Urban and Regional Research* 1 (1977): 256–271.

——. *La politique urbaine dans la région lyonnaise, 1945–1972*. Paris: Mouton, 1974.

Lowi, Theodore J. *The End of Liberalism: Ideology, Policy, and the Crisis of Public Authority*. New York: W. W. Norton and Co., 1969.

Ludwig, Richard L. "Administrative Systems for Urban Development and Renewal: The Case of Urban Renewal in France." Ph.D. dissertation, University of Pittsburgh, 1971.

McConnell, Grant. *Private Power and American Democracy*. New York: Alfred A. Knopf, 1966.

Machin, Howard. "The French Prefects and Local Administration." *Parliamentary Affairs* 27 (Summer 1974): 237–250.

McKay, David H. and Cox, Andrew W. *The Politics of Urban Change*. London: Croom Helm, 1979.

Manzoni, Herbert J. "Duddeston and Nechelles Redevelopment Areas." Report to the Birmingham Public Works Committee, May 27, 1943.

Mechain, Alain. "Réhabilitation, restauration, rénovation, restructuration: une certaine politique urbaine: analyse critique de 6 opérations." Mémoire de Troisième Cycle. University of Lyon, 1974.

Mesnard, A.-H. *La planification urbaine*. Paris: Presses Universitaires de France, 1972.

Meyerson, Martin and Banfield, Edward C. *Politics, Planning, and the Public Interest: The Case of Public Housing in Chicago*. New York: Free Press, 1955.

Milch, Jerome E. "Influence as Power: French Local Government Reconsidered." *British Journal of Political Science* 4 (April 1974): 139–162.

———. "Paris Is Not France: Policy Outputs and Political Values in Two French Cities." 2 vols. Ph.D. dissertation, Massachusetts Institute of Technology, 1973.

Mitchell, B. R. *European Historical Statistics, 1750–1970*. New York: Columbia University Press, 1975.

Monod, Jerome. *Transformation d'un pays: pour une géographie de la liberté*. Paris: Foyard, 1972.

Moynihan, Daniel P. *Coping: On the Practice of Government*. New York: Vintage Books, 1975.

Muchnick, David M. *Urban Renewal in Liverpool: A Study of the Politics of Redevelopment*. London: G. Bell & Sons, 1970.

Newton, Ken. *Second City Politics: Democratic Processes and Decision-Making in Birmingham*. London: Oxford University Press, 1976.

Paris, Chris. "Birmingham: A Study in Urban Renewal." *Centre for Environmental Studies Review* 1 (July 1977): 54–61.

Peterson, Paul E. "British Interest Group Theory Reexamined: The Politics of Comprehensive Education in Three English Cities." *Comparative Politics* 3 (April 1974): 381–402.

Peterson, Paul E. and Kantor, Paul. "Citizen Participation, Political Parties, and Democratic Theory: An Analysis of Local Politics in England." Paper presented at the 1970 annual meetings of the American Political Science Association, Los Angeles, Calif., September 1970.

Poissonier, André. *La rénovation urbaine*. Paris: Berger-Levrault, 1965.

Power, Norman S. *The Forgotten People: A Challenge to a Caring Community*. Evesham: Arthur Jones, 1965.

Pressman, Jeffrey L. and Wildavsky, Aaron. *Implementation*. Berkeley: University of California Press, 1973.

Priouret, Roger. *La Caisse des Dépôts: cent cinquante ans d'histoire financière*. Paris: Presses Universitaires de France, 1966.

Ranney, Austin. *Pathways to Parliament: Candidate Selection in Britain.* Madison: University of Wisconsin Press, 1965.

Ridley, F. F. and Blondel, Jean. *Public Administration in France.* New York: Barnes and Noble, 1969.

Rollet, M. "Bulletin municipal official de Lyon." September 30, 1968.

Rossi, Peter Henry. *The Politics of Urban Renewal: The Chicago Findings.* New York: Free Press, 1961.

Rothenberg, Jerome. *Economic Evaluation of Urban Renewal: Conceptual Foundations of Benefit-Cost Analysis.* Washington, D.C.: The Brookings Institution, 1967.

Sadek, S. E. M. *The Balance Point between Local Autonomy and National Control.* The Hague: Mouton and Co., 1972.

Sayre, Wallace S. and Kaufman, Herbert. *Governing New York City: Politics in the Metropolis.* New York: W. W. Norton and Co., 1965.

Scarrow, Howard A. "Policy Pressures by British Local Government: The Case of 'Regulation in the Public Interest.'" *Comparative Politics* 4 (October 1971): 1–28.

Schattschneider, E. E. *The Semisovereign People: A Realist's View of Democracy in America.* Hinsdale, Ill.: Dryden Press, 1975.

Sharp, Evelyn. *The Ministry of Housing and Local Government.* London: George Allen and Unwin, 1969.

Sharpe, L. James. "American Democracy Reconsidered: Part I." *British Journal of Political Science* 3 (January 1973) 1–29.

———. "American Democracy Reconsidered: Part II." *British Journal of Political Science* 3 (April 1973): 129–167.

———. *Voting in Cities: The 1964 Borough Elections.* London: Macmillan and Co., 1967.

Shonfield, Andrew. *Modern Capitalism: The Changing Balance of Public and Private Power.* London: Oxford University Press, 1970.

Shuttleworth, Brian. "Urban Renewal in Birmingham." *Labour Council Group Statement.* Shuttleworth Papers, 1972.

Smallwood, Frank. *Greater London: The Politics of Metropolitan Reform.* Indianapolis: Bobbs-Merrill Co., 1965.

Stinchcomb, Jean L. *Reform and Reaction: City Politics in Toledo.* Belmont, Calif.: Wadsworth Publishing Co., 1968.

Stone, Clarence N. *Economic Growth and Neighborhood Discontent: System Bias in the Urban Renewal Program of Atlanta.* Chapel Hill: University of North Carolina Press, 1976.

Suleiman, Ezra N. *Politics, Power, and Bureaucracy in France: The Administrative Elite.* Princeton: Princeton University Press, 1974.

Sundquist, James L. *Dispersing Population: What America Can Learn from Europe.* Washington, D.C.: The Brookings Institution, 1975.

Suttles, Gerald D. *The Social Order of the Slum.* Rev. ed. Chicago: University of Chicago Press, 1970.

Tabb, William K. and Sawers, Larry, eds. *Marxism and the Metropolis: New Perspectives in Urban Political Economy.* New York: Oxford University Press, 1978.

Tarrow, Sidney. *Between Center and Periphery: Grassroots Politicians in Italy and France.* New Haven: Yale University Press, 1977.

————. *Partisanship and Political Exchange in French and Italian Local Politics: A Contribution to the Typology of Party Systems.* Sage Professional Papers in Contemporary Western Political Sociology, vol. 1, no. 06-004. London and Beverly Hills: Sage Publications, 1974.

————. "The Urban-Rural Cleavage in Political Involvement: The Case of France." *American Political Science Review* 65 (June 1971): 341–357.

Taubman, William. *Governing Soviet Cities.* New York: Praeger Publishers, 1973.

Taylor, Ted. "Urban Renewal—The Corporate Approach." Paper presented to the Urban Renewal Seminar, Birmingham City Council, September 23, 1974.

Thoenig, Jean-Claude. *L'ère des technocrates: le cas des Ponts et chaussées.* Paris: Les Editions d'organisation, 1974.

————. "La relation entre le centre et la périphérie," *Bulletin de l'Institut International d'Administration Publique; revue d'administration publique* 36 (October-December 1975): 77–123.

United States, President's Urban and Regional Policy Group. *A New Partnership to Conserve America's Communities: A National Urban Policy.* Washington, D.C.: U.S. Government Printing Office, 1978.

Vidich, Arthur J. and Bensman, Joseph. *Small Town in Mass Society: Class, Power, and Religion in a Rural Community.* Princeton: Princeton University Press, 1968.

Warnecke, Steven J. and Suleiman, Ezra N., eds. *Industrial Policies in Western Europe.* New York: Praeger Publishers, 1975.

West Midland Group on Post-War Reconstruction and Planning. *Con-*

urbation: A Planning Survey of Birmingham and the Black Country. London: Architectural Press, 1948.

West Midlands Economic Planning Council. *The West Midlands Patterns of Growth.* London: H M S O, 1967.

Whittick, Arnold, ed. *Encyclopedia of Urban Planning.* New York: McGraw-Hill Book Company, 1974.

Williams, Philip. "Party, Presidency, and Parish Pump in France." *Parliamentary Affairs* 18 (1965): 257–265.

Wilson, James Q. *Political Organizations.* New York: Basic Books, 1973.

———, ed. *Urban Renewal: The Record and the Controversy.* Cambridge: M I T Press, 1966.

Wiseman, H. W. "The Working of Local Government in Leeds." *Public Administration* 41 (Spring 1963): 51–70.

Wolfinger, Raymond E. *The Politics of Progress.* Englewood Cliffs, N.J.: Prentice-Hall, 1974.

Wylie, Laurence. *Village in the Vaucluse.* 2d ed. Cambridge: Harvard University Press, 1964.

Yates, Douglas T. *Neighborhood Democracy: The Politics and Impacts of Decentralization.* Lexington, Mass.: Lexington Books, 1973.

———. *The Ungovernable City.* Cambridge: M I T Press, 1977.

Young, Ken. *Local Politics and the Rise of Party: The London Municipal Society and the Conservative Intervention in Local Elections.* Leicester: Leicester University Press, 1975.

Young, Michael and Willmott, Peter. *Family and Kinship in East London.* Rev. ed. Baltimore: Penguin Books, 1957.

Ysmal, Colette. "L'élection de M. Gaston Defferre à Marseille." *Revue française de science politique* 22 (April 1972): 319–347.

Index